GW00472242

LONELY SHIPS

THE SAILING SHIPS OF J. HARDIE & CO.
AND THE *ARCHIBALD RUSSELL*

LONELY SHIPS

THE SAILING SHIPS OF J. HARDIE & CO.
AND THE *ARCHIBALD RUSSELL*

H.G. Mowat

NEW CHERWELL PRESS · OXFORD

First published in Great Britain 1995
by New Cherwell Press
7 Mount Street, Oxford OX2 6DH
Copyright © 1995 H.G. Mowat

British Library Cataloguing-in-Publication Data
A catalogue record for this book
is available from the British Library

ISBN 0 9517695 8 8 (pbk)
ISBN 1 900312 05 0 (hbk)

Printed in Malta by Interprint

Contents

Acknowledgements

Chapter I The Launch   1

Chapter II The Early Years   7

Chapter III Fire and Tempest   23

Chapter IV The Keel is Laid   29

Chapter V The Ship   38

Chapter VI First Sailing   50

Chapter VII Second Voyage   62

Chapter VIII Captains Swinton and McMillan   70

Chapter IX Captain Robert Montgomery   81

Chapter X The War Years   89

Chapter XI A West Coast Voyage   104

Chapter XII Hard Times   112

Chapter XIII   Sold Foreign   127

Chapter XIV Mariehamn   137

Chapter XV Captain Karl Sjögren   144

Chapter XVI Captain Harald Lindfors   152

Chapter XVII Captain Mikael Sjögren   166

Chapter XVIII Last Voyage   181

Fleet List   190
References   206
General Index   210
Index of Ships   213
Index of Cargoes   215

List of Plates

1   The Launch of the *Archibald Russell*

                                              facing page   1

2   Captain Hardie in old age   6

3   The *Orthes*   13

4   Sydney Harbour, 1883   14

5   The *Talavera*   15

6   The *Dallam Tower* running before the storm   17

7   The *Dallam Tower* dismasted   18

8   The *Dallam Tower* under jury rig   19

9   The *Brambletye* at Narrow Quay, Bristol   20

10   The Launch of the *Hougomont*, 1897   24

11   No 11, Bothwell Street   26

12   The *Pyrenees*   28

13   The *Archibald Russell* on the stocks   30

14   After the launch   34

15   View of the poop   39

16   The *Archibald Russell*. Rigging view   43

17   Starboard side looking aft   45

18   The *Archibald Russell* under tow   48

19   The *Archibald Russell*   52

20   Iquique   54

21   Trade winds   57

22   Bowsprit view   59

23   The *Nivelle*   60

24	The *Archibald Russell*. Roaring Forties	66
25	The *Vimeira*	68
26	Captain Swinton	71
27	The *Archibald Russell* at Tacoma	72
28	The *Hougomont*	76
29	The *Chiltonford*	80
30	Captain Robert Montgomery (1879-1951)	83
31	The *Killoran*	84
32	The *Clevedon*	90
33	The *Hougomont*	92
34	Thomas G. Hardie	104
35	Sketch of Thomas G. Hardie	106
36	The *Ortina Shell*	113
37	The *Archibald Russell*. Storm conditions	119
38	The *Kilmeny*	121
39	Jansen the Swede	129
40	The sailmaker	130
41	Carroll Cundiff and shipmates	131
42	Port Lincoln	132
43	Making fast the main upper topsail	134
44	On the way to Cape Horn	135
45	The *Archibald Russell* nearing Queenstown, September 1925	136
46	Captain Gustaf Erikson	138
47	The *Hougomont* dismasted	141
48	Captain Karl Gerhard Sjögren	145
49	The *Archibald Russell* at Melbourne, 1929	147
50	Coming up channel, July 1930	149

51	Mariehamn	150
52	At the Royal Victoria Dock, London, 1931	153
53	The *Archibald Russell* photographed from the *Graf Zeppelin*	154
54	The port watch	155
55	Sailing up the Spencer Gulf, 1932	156
56	Wheat stacks at Port Augusta	158
57	After the squall	159
58	The *Archibald Russell* sailing from Wallaroo	161
59	The *Archibald Russell* in her new colours	162
60	Derelict. The hulk of the *Hougomont*	163
61	Wallaroo, 1932	164
62	The end of a long jetty	167
63	*L'Avenir* and *Winterhude* at Port Germein	169
64	The *Archibald Russell* in Bridgwater Bay, July 1937	170
65	Becalmed off Dover, September 1937	171
66	Sailing from Mariehamn	172
67	The new fore-topgallant mast	173
68	The *Penang* loading wheat at Port Germein	176
69	Heaving down the fore-tack	178
70	Stormy weather off Cape Horn	179
71	Storm damage, 1938	180
72	Coming to anchor, Falmouth Bay, 1939	183
73	Entering Hull, 1939	184
74	The *Killoran*	186
75	End of the road, 1947	189

List of Figures

1   Proposed hood over steering gear   31
2   Plan of position of bilge keels   32
3   After accommodation of the *Saragossa*   41
4   The *Archibald Russell* deck layout   44
5   The *Archibald Russell* sail plan   46
6   The s.s. *John Hardie*   63
7   Captain Buchan's track chart,
    Bordeaux to New York   96
8   Captain Buchan's track chart,
    Liverpool to Taltal   108
9   Captain Auld's track chart,
    Cowes to St Vincent   115

Acknowledgements

I am greatly indebted to a number of people whose interest in the affairs of J. Hardie & Company and their ships has helped me to compile this history.

Thanks to Mrs Ethel Hardie I was able to study all the available company documents. On the Russell family side, Mrs Marjorie James gave me every possible assistance as did Mr William S. Russell.

I am also indebted to the following organisations: the Guildhall Library which held Lloyds' records; Scotts' Shipbuilding Company Limited; C. Fox & Co. of Falmouth; the Mitchell Library, Glasgow; the Strathclyde Regional Archives where Mr Richard Dell searched so diligently for me; the Memorial University of Newfoundland; the National Maritime Museum; the Public Record Office at Chancery Lane and the Record Office of Shipping and Seamen at Llandaff; Brown, Son and Ferguson; the Cape Horners of South Australia; the United States Customs; the Ålands Sjöfartsmuseum of Mariehamn; and the Marine Society of London.

My thanks also to the editors of publications who allowed me space in their columns: *Sea Breezes*, the *Port Pirie Advertiser, Glasgow Herald, Glasgow Daily Record, Gateshead Post, Hull Daily Mail* and the *Goole Times*. Through these papers I was able to contact people who sailed in J. Hardie & Company's ships and others who were associated with them. Among these correspondents were Len Williams of Port Pirie, Ron Tilbrook, Colin Heggie, Ralph Rogerson and Claude Beneke, all Australians who sailed in the *Archibald Russell*, as did Carroll Cundiff of North Miami, Florida, Captain Raoul Rasmussen of Ontario and H. Pederson of Bornholm, Denmark. My thanks also to Captain Colin Goss and Harry Meadows of the *Hougomont* and Eben Anderson who sailed in the *Hougomont, Killoran* and *Kilmeny*. I am equally grateful to others who passed on information and lent me photographs: Nancy Robinson, the Australian authoress and journalist; Miss Dorothy Fyfe of Wallaroo; Mrs Linda Richards and Mrs Lorna Saunders of Port Pirie; Reg Mayes of Port Augusta; Mr Neil McCormack and Mr M.R. Phillips of Magnetic Island. In the United States, Captain Fred Klebingat was most helpful, also Harold Huycke and Mr James Nesdall of New York who did some useful research for me.

I had rewarding correspondence with Captain McMillan's grandson, Mr R.C. Cowan of Glasgow; also members of Captain Swinton's family, Mrs Margaret Swinton Marshall and Mr James Swinton. Captain Robert Montgomery wrote to me from Vancouver and gave me the background to the career of his father, Captain Montgomery.

Of the others who helped me I must not forget Mr Richard Cookson who gave me the benefit of his years of research into the affairs of sailing ships of the nineteenth and twentieth centuries; Mr Alex Hurst whose advice and encouragement were invaluable; Miss I.M. Underhill who allowed me to copy the plans of her brother, Mr Harold Underhill. My thanks also to Mr Michael Crowdy, Mr Harold Appleyard, Mr Graeme Somner and other members of the World Ship Society who delved for me and corresponded with me.

My thanks must also go to those who lent me photographs. I have acknowledged these where possible, but I have included one or two whose ownership I have been unable to trace. Also to Mrs M. Rodgers of Adelaide for searching out photographs for me in Australia. Finally my thanks must go to my wife Jeanne and my sister Mrs M. Burton for all the typing and indexing involved.

Plate 1 The Launch of the Archibald Russell
Scotts' Shipbuilding Co. Ltd.

Chapter I

The Launch

On January 23rd, 1905, the hull of a four-masted barque was launched from the yard of Scotts' Shipbuilding & Engineering Company at Carts-burn, Greenock.[1] This vessel was the last to be built for the firm of J. Hardie & Company which owned a substantial fleet of sailing ships. She was also the last of her class to be built in the United Kingdom.

It was a dry day but chilly and most of the people assembled on the launching dais were well wrapped up against the keen wind. The photograph of the launching party depicts about thirty-five prosperous Edwardian citizens, the men practically without exception wearing bowler hats and sporting heavy walrus moustaches, while the ladies have large hats, fur boas and long skirts which reach to the ground, with no indecent show of ankle. It is likely that the lady in the dark fur coat and hat in the foreground performed the launch and christening, and if this is the case, her name was Mrs Jackson Russell, the daughter-in-law of the late Mr Archibald Russell, a shareholder in the ships managed by J. Hardie & Co. It was a family affair as shown by the child on the extreme right of the picture. She was allowed to stand outside the balustrade to enable her to be better seen by the camera.

There is no sign of a bottle of champagne with which to christen the ship. It seems that it was not the custom of the owners to do so; maybe it was considered frivolous and wasteful, or perhaps it was not done for reasons of temperance. The Church, however, was represented by a man in clerical hat and collar to add his blessing to those of the lady who sent the ship down the ways.

Archibald Russell was the name given to the ship at this austere launching ceremony. The name was chosen to honour a close friend of Captain John Hardie, the founder of the firm. Unfortunately, neither of these two gentlemen was present at the launch, both having departed this life some time beforehand. However, Thomas and James Hardie, sons of the founder, agreed on the suggestion of the Russell family, to name the ship after the man who had been Captain Hardie's companion and business associate for many years. It has been said that a clause was entered in the Bill of Sale to the effect that the ship's name should never be changed,[2] and whether true or not, once the name was painted on her bow and stern, it remained there throughout her long life. The name and blessing she

1

received on this day as she slid down the ways carried her through 45 years, surviving storms, trade depressions, two wars and all the other hazards that man and the sea can devise.

James and Thomas Hardie, who continued to manage the firm after the death of their father five years previously, were the authors of this seemingly dour launching ceremony. In the ensuing years, numerous seamen must have been curious about the person whose name the ship bore. Although it was a sincere tribute to Mr Russell, it gave rather a sombre note to the beautiful creation, and in this the brothers departed from their usual custom of choosing places connected with Wellington's campaigns as names for their ships, such as *Talavera, Salamanca* and *Corunna*.

Mr Russell, however, was a person of some note in his own field. He was the son of one of the early pioneers in opening up the Scottish coalfields, and after the death of his father he expanded his mining interests, becoming one of the largest colliery owners in West Scotland. He was the Chairman of the Lanarkshire & Dumbartonshire Railway Company, Director of the Lanarkshire & Ayrshire Railway Company and Director Extraordinary of the Commercial and Union Banks. He was also a founder partner of the Clutha Shipping Company. He was survived by four sons and two daughters.[3]

Mr Archibald Russell may have been the driving force behind the formation of the Clutha Shipping Company, but it was his friend, Captain Hardie, whose knowledge of ships and their management made it a profitable venture.

John Hardie was born in Glasgow in 1836, a year before Queen Victoria came to the throne. He grew up at a time when there were great changes taking place in the affairs of shipping, and in a city which was giving more than any other towards the development of ships and the expansion of trade throughout the world. The emergence of the clipper ship, the use of iron construction and the particular interest of Scottish engineers in the marine steam engine brought Glasgow to her peak in the shipping industry in the nineteenth century.

With shipping so influencing the people of Glasgow, it is not surprising that the young John Hardie embarked on a seagoing career at the age of thirteen by signing on the ship *Cressida* in 1849 for a voyage to India. This was possibly a trial voyage to see whether his heart was in it, but his mind remained unchanged, and on his return he signed an indenture apprenticing himself to George Smith junior, a Glasgow shipowner and partner of the firm of George Smith and Sons. This was a contract of a standard form which thousands of youths before him and many more thereafter signed, binding themselves for a period of four years during which they would hand, reef and steer and do any other work, however menial, required aboard ship. In return for the sum of £26 for the four years, the Master of the ship agreed to teach him the business of a seaman which would, if the young man turned out to be diligent, eventually lead him to command. There were provisos in young Hardie's indenture, one of them being a penalty of £10 to be paid by his uncle James Hardie, who signed the indenture, as surety in case the contract was not honoured; and another demanding that if the boy should join the Royal Navy, which he was entitled to do if his patriotic duty called him, any 'Wages, Prize-money and other Moneys' should become the property of the shipowner.[4]

John, now fourteen years old, joined Smiths' *City of London*, a full-rigged ship, on voyages to India. It was an adventurous life through oceans still incompletely explored or charted, where pirates and privateers still sailed. New Zealand was just starting to be colonised and Britain had only ceased to send convicts to Botany Bay ten years previously. In the Far East, Japan was still a country of great mystery, forbidden to Westerners. He served his four years in the *City of London* and is described in a reference by the Master, Captain Albert Blair, as a 'steady industrious young man who knows his business'.[5] In 1856 he was Second Mate of the *City of Dublin* for two Indian voyages, followed by two more as First Mate; on leaving the ship in 1859 he sat for his Master's ticket, and on passing was granted Certificate of Competency No 12557. On the strength of this, Smiths gave him command of his old ship the *City of London*.[6]

1861 found him wanting a change. The reason probably was his marriage, as he wrote in a letter to his owners that he wanted shorter voyages; accordingly he left Smiths and joined the British and North American Royal Mail Steam Packet Company, but he had to start at the bottom again as Fourth Mate on the s/s *Asia*. By 1862 he had only risen to Third Mate, but by then he had had enough of the Company, or perhaps he had decided he did not like steamers; so he returned to his old firm who were pleased to have him back and gave him command of the *City of Calcutta*.

The opening of the Suez Canal in 1869 caused shipowners to consider seriously the advantage of steamships in the Far Eastern trade and in 1870 we find John Hardie in command of one of Smiths' first steamships, the *City of Oxford*, in which he made one of the earliest transits of the Canal. After a spell in command of the *City of Manchester* he was again looking for a change; in fact from correspondence it appears that he was finding that the loneliness on the long voyages away from his wife and family, now increased by two boys and four girls, had become hard to bear. This is borne out by some poems on loneliness found among his private logbooks.[7] In 1874, Smiths' ship's husband sent him a confidential letter saying that he was leaving, suggesting that he might be interested in his job. When he was eventually offered it, John Hardie 'swallowed the anchor' for good. A ship's husband was a more humble name for what is now known as a Marine Superintendent, the person who looks after the maintenance and manning of the ships.

It was during this period that John Hardie became acquainted with Mr Russell. On April 19th, 1876, both men were present at a meeting held at the counting house of Mr George Wallace in Exchange Square, Glasgow, where proposals were drawn up and directors appointed in order to form a copartnery, which was to be called the Clutha Shipping Company, for the purchase and sale of vessels and the employment of same. The capital involved was £60,000 divided into shares of £100. Mr Russell was in the Chair; the other people involved included Glasgow citizens with useful contacts in business such as steel and iron, shipbuilding, banking and insurance. Captain Hardie was appointed Manager and authorised to undertake the building of three ships, which were to be British built, of iron or composite construction and to the highest standard of the time. It was agreed that the names of the first two ships should be *Inch Moan* and *Inch Colm* and that the salary of their Masters should be £15 per month and two and a half per cent of the net profits. It was expected that reasonable profits would be made and that there would be an annual dividend; but in the event of a loss by the ships, it was understood that the shareholders would bear the cost and square the account.

The parties present at this meeting who undertook to put up the capital were as follows:

Mr Archibald Russell	Coalmaster	£8,000
Mr James Napier	Manufacturer	£8,000
Mr Thomas Arnot	Warehouseman	£8,000
Messrs Wingate, Birrell & Co.	Insurance Brokers	£8,000
Mr Hugh Neilson	Ironmaster	£8,000
Captain James Adams		£4,000
Mr Francis Watson	Baker and Confectioner	£4,000
Captain John Hardie	Merchant	£4,000

The shares which were not taken up at the time were later divided amongst those eager to purchase more stock in the company. Captain Hardie formed his own company, J. Hardie & Co., to deal with the management of the ships. For Captain Hardie, it was a matter of changing from superintending Smiths' ships to doing the same for those of the Clutha Shipping Company in which he now had a financial interest.[8]

Three ships were ordered from the firm of D. & W. Henderson & Co. of Glasgow. The first two were barques of 780 and 787 net tons respectively and built of iron. When they were launched, they were named *Inch Moan* and *Inch Marnock*, the name of the latter having been changed for some reason. The third vessel, also of iron, was a full-rigged ship of 1,074 net tons and named the *Inch Kenneth*. Mr Birrell arranged the insurance of the two barques which were valued at £13,000, the contract price being £15.10s on their gross tonnage. The whole project was very much in the spirit of the merchant venturers of old, with the shareholders able to purchase goods and merchandise in order to provide a cargo, or part of one, although to what extent they did this is not known and it is likely that Captain Hardie and the ships' Masters negotiated most of the cargoes. Certainly they were prepared to send their ships to any part of the world where there was the possibility of obtaining a profitable cargo, and by the end of the summer of 1876 the three ships were outward bound: the *Inch Moan* to Chile and the *Inch Marnock* and the *Inch Kenneth* to India.

Affairs started uncomfortably for the new company in the first twelve months. The *Inch Moan* went ashore on the coast of Chile and was wrecked, and the *Inch Kenneth* foundered on the homeward passage from Calcutta. The *Inch Marnock*, under Captain Robson, one of the firm's most successful Masters, completed her outward voyage but struck an uncharted rock when entering Rangoon and was delayed while the damage was repaired. Fortunately the ships were well covered by insurance, although in the case of the *Inch Marnock* it was decided to pay for the repairs out of funds. In spite of these setbacks the first year's trading showed a profit, and a dividend of £10 per share was distributed to the shareholders. Captain Hardie, who had set up his place of business at 18, Renfield Place, Glasgow, received for his services £100 per ship per annum to cover the cost of management, and two and a half per cent of the net profits.

In 1879, the losses had not only been replaced but the number of vessels had been increased to five full-rigged ships: the *Inch Marnock*, the *Inch Keith*, the *Inch Murren*, the *Salamanca* and the *Orthes*; and for the next five years the company earned substantial profits. The shareholders received dividends of between seven and ten per cent, the balance going into the reserve fund. 1885 to 1887 were lean years which may have been partly due to one of the first trade depressions that were to plague the shipping industry every decade for years to come, or the fact that considerable

5

120 BUCHANAN ST.
GLASGOW
AND HELENSBURGH.

Plate 2   Captain Hardie in old age
Mrs Ethel Hardie

expense had been incurred over the two new vessels built for them, the *Talavera* in 1882 and the *Albuera* in 1885. The *Talavera*, built of iron, had the distinction of being the firm's first four-masted barque, while the *Albuera*, a full-rigged ship, was unusual in the fact that she was built of steel which made for lighter construction and improved carrying capacity over ships of similar size built of iron.

Mr Russell resigned as Managing Director of the Clutha Shipping Company in favour of Captain Hardie, although he continued to chair the meetings. Other shareholders, including Mr Birrell, left the company due to death or resignation and Captain Hardie, who had added insurance broking to his business, now handled the insurance of the ships. He also purchased further stock in the company. His sons, James and Thomas, came into the business and his brother, Captain James Hardie, acquired fifty-five of the late Mr Arnot's shares. The Clutha Shipping Company was now dominated by the Hardie family and the name became eclipsed by that of J. Hardie & Company, who were generally considered as the owners of the ships. Captain John Hardie and Mr Archibald Russell remained close friends until the former's death in 1899. They both shared a love of sailing ships and there is no doubt that Mr Russell's interests in the coal industry were very useful in securing profitable outward cargoes for their vessels.

Chapter II

The Early Years

In the early days of the Clutha Shipping Company, cargoes were sought in the Far East where Captain Hardie had traded during his years with the ships of Smiths' City Line. The *Inch Keith*, the *Inch Murren*, the *Orthes*, the *Talavera* and the *Dallam Tower*, of whose adventures we shall hear more later, were frequently to be seen loading in Calcutta, Bombay, Rangoon and Chittagong. In time, steamships moved in on the market, taking over the bulk of the trade. This meant that the ships had to seek trade further east in the Dutch East Indies ports of Batavia and Sourabaya or the remote anchorages in any of the islands where cargoes could be found. Bangkok and Saigon were visited and occasionally the harbours of Reunion and Mauritius. The *Salamanca* and the *Inch Marnock* traded to Australia, mainly to Sydney and Adelaide. They also visited the New Zealand ports of Lyttelton and Wellington.

By 1890, the Far Eastern trade had dwindled for sailing ships, and Hardies' big barques were seeking nitrate cargoes at the ports of Chile and Peru or grain from San Francisco, to Europe. The turn of the century saw their ships tramping all over the world looking for profitable cargoes, but the emphasis was on coal outward to South America and nitrates home, or alternatively, intermediate passages across the Pacific to Australia for coal back to Chile, or grain for the United Kingdom.

The ships of the Clutha Shipping Company were well found, and although they were not numbered amongst the clipper ships they often made passages equal to the best known ships of those days. They also suffered a number of adventures, misfortunes and fatalities. The significance of their passage times can only be judged by comparing them with contemporary vessels with established reputations for speed. Captain Woodget's voyages in the *Cutty Sark* in the Australian trade are well documented and although not the fastest, serve as a comparison. On his first voyage in 1885, he sailed her out from the Lizard to Sydney Heads in 73 days and home again in 77. These were fast passages and although the *Cutty Sark* did better with 70 days in 1888, her average over the years was in excess of 80.[1] We shall see that some of the Clutha Shipping Company's vessels matched these times.

In the trade between the United Kingdom and the Indian continent, a passage of 100 days would be rated a fair one. The *Inch Keith* and the

Orthes improved on this occasionally and the *Talavera* quite frequently. To the South American ports, the full-rigged ship *Glenalvon* is credited with 34 days from Liverpool to Rio and Captain Hardie's Movement Book shows that the *Salamanca* came near this with 35. In voyages westward round Cape Horn to ports in Chile and Peru, the British four-masted barque *Eudora*, with a fine reputation for speed, is credited with 71 days to Callao from Barry, but most shipowners would be satisfied with between 90 and 100 days on both outward and homeward passages. Two of the fastest trans-Pacific passages outwards appear to have been those of the four-masted barques *Wendur* and *Loch Torridon*, which together raced from Newcastle, N.S.W. to Valparaiso in 29 days in 1896.[2]

In estimating a sailing ship's time between ports, a daily average of 120 miles per day was considered fair. Luck with the wind and weather played a great part in the making of an outstanding passage, but it also required a determined Captain and a competent crew. Without these three factors, nothing special was likely to be achieved.

The *Inch Marnock*, it will be remembered, hit a rock entering Rangoon Harbour on her maiden voyage, after which she was repaired and resumed her passage. She had a short life of only ten years, spent mainly in the colonial trade to Australia and New Zealand. With three masts and barque rig, she was not as fast as the full-rigged ships or four-masted barques which followed, more of a steady passage-maker, but her first Master was a man who seemed to be able to get more out of a ship than most. His name was Robson and under him her best passages were:

| 1877 | Glasgow | to | Adelaide | 88 days |
| 1878 | London | to | Wellington | 87 days |

Captain Robson left in 1879 to take over the *Salamanca*. The *Inch Marnock*'s next Master was Captain A.J. Petrie. He was a young man in his twenties and this was his first voyage in command, having previously been First Mate of the *Salamanca* under Captain Sage. The voyage commenced well with a 90 day passage from Glasgow to Adelaide, followed by an exceptionally quick turnaround by Hardies' agents, Messrs Harrold Bros., in three weeks and three days, during which her cargo was discharged and 10,295 bags of wheat loaded. The details of the events which followed are taken from an Adelaide newspaper dated February 7th, 1880, the name of which unfortunately is not included in the cutting, headed 'The Stranding of the Barque *Inch Marnock*'.

The *Inch Marnock* sailed from Adelaide at about noon on Tuesday, February

8

3rd, her destination Falmouth. The weather was apparently cold for the time of year and the wind was southerly, described as a 'leading' wind for the *Inch Marnock*, which was able to make a good course westward down Investigator Strait. At 9.30 that evening, Captain Petrie picked up Marsden Point on Kangaroo Island, distant nine and a half miles, and with the wind free enough to make a good course for the open sea, all appeared to be going well, with the barque on the port tack making good speed. He expected to see the light on Althorpe Island, situated on the southern tip of Yorke Peninsula, and this should have appeared on the starboard bow, but as time went on and there was no sign of the light, he climbed to the fore-topsail yard for a better view and remained aloft until 1.00 am without seeing anything. On returning to the deck, he sighted the coastline of Foul Bay to leeward and realised that the *Inch Marnock* was far closer to the land than he anticipated and in great danger. Calling all hands out to bring her to the other tack, the helm was put hard down and the barque came up into the wind, but at the critical time she missed stays, lost headway and started to drift shoreward. The starboard anchor was hurriedly dropped, but it was too late and she grounded aft, at the same time listing over to port.

The situation was bad but not hopeless. After sounding all round, Captain Petrie found the *Inch Marnock*'s stern to be resting on a sandbank with her forward part in deeper water. However, it was clear that she was not going to be got off without help, and if that wasn't available while the weather remained comparatively fine, it was likely that she would stay there for good. He ordered a boat to be launched and landed the Second Mate who was sent off with two men to walk overland to the nearest telegraph station at Woororo to send a message to Harrold Bros. informing them of the stranding and to obtain the assistance of a tug. It was 4.00 am and still dark when the shore party set off. One of them had been instructed to return to the ship and report their progress, but unfortunately they got lost in the bush.

Daylight revealed that the *Inch Marnock* lay two miles north-east of Yorke Point about a mile from the rugged and unfriendly coast. Under the circumstances, the Captain must have wondered why the ship ended up there and whether his compasses were faulty or the set of the current was stronger than he anticipated. Anyway, since no word had come back from the shore party to say whether they had succeeded in getting in touch with Adelaide, Captain Petrie, impatient to get things moving, set off in a boat for Port Moorowie on the far side of Sturt Bay, some fourteen miles distant. He took two men with him and had a rough sail, during which they were nearly swamped by the heavy swell.

It was five o'clock on Wednesday evening when Messrs Harrold Bros., in Adelaide, received a message that the Inch *Marnock* was ashore. Any nautical affairs were always of great interest around the waterfront and by 10.00 pm the tug *Yatala* was on her way to Foul Bay with a crowd of people which included Mr John Clark of Harrold Bros., members of the press, representatives of Lloyds' underwriters, the local Receiver of Wrecks, officials of the Adelaide Harbour Authority and customs officers. They set off at the *Yatala*'s best speed which was about six knots, arriving at Foul Bay at 9.00 am on Thursday morning. There were two Master Mariners on board, and in consultations with Captain Petrie it was decided to start jettisoning cargo from the after hold. Some of the crew were set about this task while others were ordered aloft to send down the topgallant and royal yards because the pounding which the barque was getting from the swell was weakening the rigging and threatening to bring down the masts. The *Inch Marnock*'s port anchor, with a heavy steel wire attached to it, was carried out with the help of the *Yatala* and dropped 500 feet to seaward, and the hauling part taken to the capstan on the fo'c'sle head in readiness to assist heaving the ship off when the time came. The *Yatala* was then despatched to Port Moorowie to get a barge to take some of her cargo, and a passing steamer, the *Flinders*, on her way from Port Augusta to Adelaide, was asked to make a request for another tug.

Meanwhile, affairs were looking better. 313 bags of wheat had been thrown overboard and when the *Yatala* returned from Port Moorowie, it was thought by those on board the *Inch Marnock* that there was a good chance of her coming off. At five o'clock the *Yatala* made fast and the tow began. For an hour there was no perceptible change in her position but with the help of the crew straining at the windlass, she finally slid off into deep water and was towed clear. The port anchor was slipped and the *Yatala* commenced the tow back to Adelaide, arriving at Semaphore Point seventeen hours later, at noon on the Friday.

The *Inch Marnock* had sustained some damage during her 40 hours ashore, and it was four weeks before she was ready to sail. This was particularly galling to Harrold Bros., who had made such an effort to give her a speedy turnaround. None the less, the voyage was completed in eight months and sixteen days, among the best times recorded and beaten only by Captain Robson in the *Salamanca* and the *Talavera*. The *Inch Marnock* came home via the Cape of Good Hope in 101 days, reporting at St Helena on the way. Captain Petrie remained one more voyage and then went on to command the *Inch Murren*.

Captain Petrie was followed by Captain True, who displeased the shareholders with his lengthy passages, the worst during his period in command being 186 days from Bassein, a port just north of Bombay, to Falmouth in

1883. He was asked to resign, his place being taken by Mr McDonald who was the First Mate at the time.[3] McDonald started off well on his first outward voyage. He was 18 days from the Scillies to the Line and 94 to Bundaberg in Queensland, followed by 44 days from Newcastle, N.S.W., in ballast to Valparaiso. The *Inch Marnock* then sailed homewards to Falmouth in 114 days. On his second voyage, his passages were:

1885	Rotterdam	to	Port Pirie	91 days
	Port Pirie	to	Sourabaya	36 days
	Sourabaya	to	Falmouth	128 days

On her next voyage, the *Inch Marnock* was 103 days to Batavia and after calling at Sourabaya and Pekalongan, she sailed for home but foundered in bad weather on January 25th, 1887, off Algoa Bay. Although the ship *Sydenham* picked up the survivors and landed them at Cape Town, Captain McDonald was not among them.

The *Salamanca* and the *Orthes* were sister ships and came from the same yard of Messrs James and George Thomson of Glasgow. The tendency was for larger ships. Their net tonnage was 1,202 and 1,206 respectively. The *Salamanca*, a full-rigged ship, was a consistently good passage-maker; she was 110 days from San Francisco to Queenstown on her maiden voyage under Captain Sage, and 92 days from London to Adelaide in the following year, but she really did not show her paces until Captain Robson took command in 1879. It was in the *Salamanca* that he earned a name as a fast passage-maker. On his first voyage, she ran out to Sydney from Glasgow in 82 days and then came home again from Port Lyttelton in New Zealand in 84 days. On the next voyage in 1880-1881, she went from London to Sydney and back in 7 months and 27 days, no time at all being wasted on this round trip which was an unusually quick one. Her best passage times were:

1880	London	to	Sydney	82 days
1881	Sydney	to	London	97 days

On the third and last voyage of the *Salamanca* under Captain Robson, she made a fast passage of 79 days from London to Sydney. Captain Robson left to take over the newly built *Talavera*, his place being taken by Captain Bryce who, up until then, had been the *Salamanca*'s First Mate. During Captain Bryce's nine years in command, he did well with her.

1883	London	to	Rio de Janeiro	35 days

1883	London	to	Calcutta	106 days
1884	London	to	Calcutta	103 days
1886	San Francisco	to	Queenstown	115 days
1888	London	to	Sydney	83 days
1889	London	to	Auckland	93 days

Captain Williams came next. He was equally successful with her during his four years in command.

1892	Glasgow Newcastle	to	Sydney	82 days
	N.S.W.	to	Iquique	38 days
	Iquique	to	Falmouth	87 days
1894	Glasgow Newcastle	to	Sydney	81 days
	N.S.W.	to	Valparaiso	33 days
1896	Sydney	to	Valparaiso	37 days

On the *Salamanca*'s last voyage for the Clutha Shipping Company, she made one of her best passages. There was another change of Master this voyage, Captain Williams being replaced by Captain Robertson. It was the only time he sailed with the Company as Master, but under him she ran out from Liverpool to Melbourne in 76 days. On her return she was sold to Italian buyers.

The full-rigged ship *Orthes* was launched seven months after her sister ship the *Salamanca*. As far as passage-making is concerned, there was little to choose between the two vessels. In 1880, the *Orthes* sailed from London to Canterbury, New Zealand in 90 days and home again in 80. The following year, she made the round voyage from London to Calcutta and back in 7 months and 28 days. Her voyages in the Indian trade were altogether very regular and satisfactory, in fact she never made a poor one. When this trade was lost to the steamships she went tramping, sometimes to the Indonesian Archipelago and other times to Australia and South America. Over the years she achieved some good passages:

1888	Liverpool	to	Valparaiso	78 days
1892	London	to	Adelaide	83 days
			(77 days from the Lizard)	
1893	Newport	to	Montevideo	44 days
1894	Newcastle N.S.W.	to	Valparaiso	46 days

Plate 3   The Orthes
A.D. Edwardes Collection, State Library of South Australia

In 1897, she was sold out of the Company to Norwegian owners and renamed *Mataura*.

The *Inch Keith* and the *Inch Murren*, built in 1878, were full-rigged ships. They were both steady passage-makers. In nineteen years, the *Inch Keith* only did one bad passage, 146 days from Calcutta to Dundee in 1886. Most of the time she traded between the United Kingdom and Indian ports, her best passages being under the first Master, Captain Peebles. In 1888, he sailed her out of Cardiff to Calcutta in 82 days. She was sold in 1897 to Italian buyers and reduced to barque rig.

The *Inch Murren*'s life with Hardies was a short one. Captain Petrie came from the *Inch Marnock* to command her from 1881 until her end, and under him she did her best passages:

1883	Glasgow	to	Sydney	88 days
1885	Ardrossan	to	Madras	88 days
	Antwerp	to	Melbourne	82 days
1886	Antwerp	to	Melbourne	81 days

In 1888, she ran out from Liverpool to Iquique in 91 days. On her home-

13

Plate 4 Sydney Harbour 1883
A.F. Peters

ward passage she caught fire and had to be abandoned on November 24th, in Latitude 14°41'S, Longitude 35°13'W. The crew were landed at Rio de Janeiro by the barque *Baltimore.*

The *Talavera* was Captain Hardie's own venture and she was registered in his name. He opted for a large vessel with four masts and barque rig, so much more suitable for the increased length. She was a beautiful ship, built of iron by Birrell, Stenhouse & Co., of Dumbarton, in 1882, and was a forerunner of the series of similar barques which the Hardies were to acquire over the next few years and which proved so successful. She was fitted with the old style bowsprit and jibboom and also single topgallants, both of which were still the rule rather than the exception. Her masts had a pleasing rake, giving the impression of the fast ship which she proved herself to be. Her main deck was uncluttered, having only one house which was placed just abaft the mainmast and contained the donkey-boiler and galley. The seamen lived before the mast under the topgallant fo'c'sle, which was their traditional place of abode, albeit a rather uncomfortable one. There was a teak charthouse on the poop with a stairway down to the accommodation below, where the Master and officers lived.

The *Talavera* earned a reputation for being a fast ship under the redoubtable Captain Robson, who commanded her from her maiden voyage until 1893. One of her most outstanding passages under him was 73 days from London to Melbourne in 1888, during which she ran from the Lizard to the Line in 22 days. Captain Hardie's Movement Book gives, amongst others, the following passages:

1885	London	to	Calcutta	85 days
1886	London	to	Melbourne	89 days
1890	Algoa	to	Lyttelton	30 days
1891	London	to	Sydney	85 days
1892	Newcastle			
	N.S.W.	to	Valparaiso	37 days
	Iquique	to	Falmouth	92 days

In 1886, the *Talavera* was matched for a short while with the *Cutty Sark*. She sailed from London on February 16th, one day before the clipper, and was still ahead of her at Start Point. She reached the Equator in 34 days as opposed to the *Cutty Sark's* 37. By the time she reached the Cape of Good Hope, the *Cutty Sark* had caught up, passing the Cape on the same day. But while this shows that the *Talavera* had a good turn of speed, it must be

Plate 5 The Talavera
A.D. Edwardes Collection, State Library of South Australia

15

pointed out that the *Cutty Sark* was not at her best being deep loaded with scrap iron. Soon after passing the Cape they parted company, the *Cutty Sark* bearing away for Anjer while the *Talavera* went on to Melbourne, arriving 89 days out.[4]

Captain Robson left the *Talavera* in 1893 to command the *Corunna*. His place was taken by Captain McCleave. In 1895, the *Talavera* loaded a part cargo of coal and general at Newcastle, N.S.W., and sailed for Valparaiso on February 12th. After discharging part of her cargo there, she set sail with the balance for Talcahuano, 330 miles down the coast. Because of the prevailing winds and current on the coast of Chile, a sailing vessel intending to fetch up at a point to the south of her port of departure, had to make a wide detour to the west before setting course for her destination. The *Talavera* left Valparaiso on April 15th and sixteen days later, on May 1st, when making her anchorage, ran ashore near Santa Maria Island just south of Talcahuano. There was dense fog at the time and she stranded on a sandbank at high water. At first there appeared some possibility that she might be salvaged. She remained upright but was so far up on the bank that, at low water, it was possible to walk right round her. The cargo was discharged but all attempts to float her were unsuccessful and she was abandoned.

After the success of the *Talavera* with her four-masted rig and larger tonnage, there seems to be no apparent reason why the Company chose to build another full-rigged ship of only 1,502 tons. No doubt the *Albuera* was a successful ship and a good dividend earner, but she was a plodder, tramping far and wide and looking through her records it is hard to find a passage of any particular note, although this does not detract from the ship's worth in any way, for at least she seems to have had a trouble-free life. Captain Steven, her first Master, came to her from the *Inch Keith*. He was a Scot and was described by one of his apprentices in Basil Lubbock's *Last of the Windjammers* as 'a lean, keen, pretty-mannered man, more like a clever sort of doctor to look at than a sailor'. Whatever one makes of this description of him, he was a fine seaman and served Hardies well for 21 years, later going to the *Vimiera*, the *Saragossa* and the *Nivelle*. On the *Albuera*'s maiden voyage, she was 150 days from Glasgow to San Francisco and 122 days on her return to Limerick. The only two passages worthy of mention under Captain Steven are:

| 1888 | London | to | Sydney | 94 days |
| 1889 | Cardiff | to | Rio de Janeiro | 44 days |

Plate 6 The Dallam Tower *running before the storm*
A.D. Edwardes Collection, State Library of South Australia

Captain Wyness followed Captain Steven and in 1891, on his second voyage, he brought the *Albuera* out from London to Sydney in 96 days, followed by 51 days from Newcastle, N.S.W. to Mollendo in Peru. Captains Gomm, Mason, Walker and Reynolds did their best, but never coaxed any fast passages from her. In 1911, she was sold to Thomas Brovig of Farsund, Norway.

The full-rigged ship *Dallam Tower* was not built for the Clutha Shipping Company but came under Captain Hardie's management on behalf of her owner, J. Forrester, in 1885. She is worth a few lines because, when under the ownership of the Lancaster Shipowners' Company earlier in her career, she was totally dismasted down south in the Indian Ocean and had to make the rest of the way to Melbourne, a matter of 2,000 miles under jury rig, which was no mean feat.

She had left London in May 1873, bound for Australia with cargo and passengers. In mid-July she was in the Roaring Forties, 300 miles south-west of Cape Leeuwin, running before a heavy gale and taking a severe beating. The seas broke over her decks, carrying away the standard compass, lifeboats, a deck cargo of livestock and the saloon skylight, causing the accommodation to be flooded out. It appears that she should have been

17

DALLAM TOWER. STORM AT IT'S HEIGHT.

Plate 7 The Dallam Tower *dismasted*
A.D. Edwardes Collection, State Library of South Australia

hove-to at the onset of the storm but the Captain, anxious to make a fast passage, had left it too late. When the decision was finally taken to bring the ship to the wind, she went right over on to her beam ends and lay there until the fore-topmast and main and mizzen topgallant masts were cut away. This saved her, but before the storm blew itself out the remaining spars went overboard, leaving her a shattered, mastless hulk. Somehow the crew managed to rig jury masts with spare spars and set what sail they could on stunsail booms, but it took them 36 days to make the remaining 2,000 miles to Port Phillip Bay. In spite of the ship being washed out fore and aft, together with all the dangers of falling spars, no members of the crew nor any passengers were lost or suffered any real injury. Such feats of seamanship were not uncommon in the days of sail. [5]

After this she was re-rigged and resumed trading, joining the Hardie fleet in 1889. She did three voyages under Captain Hardie's management and on the first, with Captain Howie in command, she ran out to Sydney from Glasgow in 83 days and thence to Bombay when, after loading, she sailed to Dunkirk in 113. Captain Williamson then took command and there followed a rather lengthy passage of 112 days from Glasgow to Sydney. She took on a coal cargo further up the coast at Newcastle, N.S.W.,

18

for Sourabaya, loading for home at several ports in the Indonesian Archipelago. Her next two passages under Captain Williamson were:

1888	Penarvekan	to	Greenock	122 days
	Glasgow	to	Sydney	98 days

This voyage was intended to follow the pattern of the previous one and she again went to Newcastle, N.S.W. for coal, sailing in early January, 1889 for a remote destination on the coast of Java recorded as Probolingo, but on the way there she stranded on a reef which in Captain Hardie's Movement Book is given as being off Cape Sloko, 'about 185 miles from Sourabaya', somewhere in the region of the entrance to Lombok Strait, close by the island of Bali. The stranding occurred on April 18th, 1889, and five days later the crew abandoned her.

There only remain two ships of this period not mentioned: the *Aberlemno* and the *Brambletye*, neither of which was built for the Clutha Shipping Company. The *Aberlemno*, a barque of 750 tons net, was built in 1876 by Birrell, Stenhouse & Co., for D.T. Boyd of Glasgow. She came under Hardies' management in 1885 and features in their Movement Book for

Plate 8 The Dallam Tower *under jury rig*
A.D. Edwardes Collection, State Library of South Australia

Plate 9 The Brambletye *at Narrow Quay, Bristol*
Keen Collection, Bristol Museum & Art Gallery

two voyages to 1888, the first of which took her on a leisurely passage of 17 months and 28 days to the River Plate, Ceylon, Bangkok and British Columbia. Her Master on this voyage was Captain Clark who was in no hurry as the passages show:

Glasgow	to	Ensenada	58 days
Ensenada	to	Galle	67 days
Galle	to	Bangkok	36 days
Bangkok	to	Victoria B.C.	78 days
Victoria B.C.	to	London	162 days

The second voyage under a new Master, Captain Connon, lasted 11 months and 8 days to the Dutch East Indies, outward to Batavia in 115 days and home to Queenstown from Sourabaya in 147. Her next owner was M. Tutton of Swansea. He had her until 1905 when she was sold to Norway.

The *Brambletye* was built for W.R. Price of Glasgow in 1876. She had two changes of ownership before coming into the Hardie fleet, the first being W. & J. Crawford followed by J. Hay of Glasgow. She was a full-rigged ship of 1,495 tons net, having a remarkably deep bar keel of 12 ins;[6] this may have made her a weatherly ship but she was not a flyer, rather more of a steady voyager, although during the nineteen years that Hardies managed her she occasionally produced a reasonably good passage. On her first voyage for them in 1890, she was 96 days from London to Sydney. She then took a coal cargo from Newcastle, N.S.W. to Lyttelton, sailing home from there to London in 104 days, a satisfactory voyage of 10 months and 25 days, having carried three cargoes with no long ballast passages between ports. This was her shortest voyage in the Movement Book. The Master for this voyage and the following one was Captain Malcolm. On the second voyage, she was 97 days from London to Sydney. She went on to Rangoon and Rio de Janeiro, then westward round Cape Horn to Talcahuano for nitrate, and home from there to Queenstown in the excellent time of 86 days.

The third voyage was an exceptionally long one lasting 3 years and 4 months during which she thrice circled the globe and rounded the Horn three times. Captain Malcolm's place was taken by Captain Dicks. She sailed from Newport to Rio to Janeiro with coal in 42 days, a very fair passage. Captain Dicks left here, no reason given, and was replaced by Captain Gomm. The voyage continued:

1894	Rio de Janeiro	to	Newcastle N.S.W.	75 days
	Newcastle N.S.W.	to	Carrizal (Chile)	56 days
1895	Carrizal	to	Philadelphia	101 days
	Philadelphia	to	Yokohama	169 days
1896	Yokohama	to	Tacoma	29 days
	Tacoma	to	Algoa Bay	101 days
	Algoa Bay	to	Semaphore (S. Australia)	37 days

The call at Semaphore was for orders and she went from there to Sydney. After loading, she sailed home to London in 94 days. Captain Gomm left her to join the *Albuera*.

The *Brambletye*'s next Master was Captain Jones. In 1900, she came to Algoa Bay from London in 73 days and was taken over as a Government store ship at the tail end of the Boer War, swinging at anchor for eight months. In 1901, she commenced another long tramping voyage of 34 months under Captain Mullen, calling at the following ports: Gothenberg -

Melbourne - Newcastle N.S.W. - Portland (Oregon) - Port Natal - Buenos Aires - Sydney - Newcastle N.S.W. - Caldera - Iquique - Sydney again and home to Falmouth in 110 days. During this long voyage, the only passage of note was 39 days from Newcastle N.S.W. to Caldera.

Captain Dobson had her for the last three voyages, shorter ones now and for the next five years, she plodded sedately round the world. In 1909, she came home from Santa in Peru in 147 days to Plymouth. She was now in her 35th year and nearing the end of her days. A tug took her in tow on February 10th for Antwerp, which was to be her last port of call. She seemed reluctant to make the final passage and the tug, after battling against head winds of gale force for two days, was forced to bring her back to Plymouth. They sailed again three days later, arriving at Antwerp on February 18th, 1909. Soon after this she was sold for scrap.

In 1891, Hardies' office was moved to new premises at 12, Waterloo Street.[7] Times were changing, new ships were needed, ships with increased carrying capacity built for bulk cargoes which were becoming the sailing ship's lot, the cream of the cargoes now going to steamships. Plans were drawn up for three four-masted barques of 2,160 tons net, a size which proved to be an economic one and yet not too large to be unhandy under sail. Speed to a certain extent might be sacrificed but this was inevitable. Anyway, the day of the tea and wool clippers was over.

Chapter III

Fire and Tempest

The first of the new series was the *Vimeira*, built at Glasgow by C. Connell & Co., and launched in July, 1891. Her tonnage was 2,163 net and her measurements 283.4 ft by 24.7 ft. She was rigged with single topgallant yards and altogether differed in looks very little from the *Talavera*, except that Connells had dispensed with the jibboom, giving her a long, tapering spar which was called a spike boom, usually referred to as a bowsprit. The *Pyrenees*, which was launched a few weeks later, was a sister ship and almost identical, differing only in size by 6 tons. She also came from Connells' yard. The five ships which followed after were the *Corunna*, from the yard of D. & W. Henderson & Co., in 1893, the *Nivelle* and the *Hougomont* from Scotts' Shipbuilding & Engineering Co., in 1897, the *Saragossa* built by the Dundee Shipbuilders' Co., of Dundee, in 1902 and finally the *Archibald Russell* in 1905, the last sailing ship built by Scotts. They were all ten feet longer than the *Vimeira* and the *Pyrenees*, and larger by 100 tons.

The launch of the *Hougomont* was the last at which Captain Hardie was present. He died on May 27th, 1899, leaving a successful and well-run organisation with the foundation of the modern fleet of ships truly laid. The new ships were conservative in design and few changes were made or innovations tried out. An invention by a Scottish shipmaster, Captain J.C. Jarvis of Tayport, for bracing a sailing ship's yards mechanically, was considered; this was to make it possible to change from one tack to another by leading the braces to winches which were cranked manually by a few hands, reducing the number of seamen normally required for the manoeuvre. Plans were drawn up for the winches to be installed on the *Saragossa*, but for some reason they were never implemented, although they proved successful in other ships, notably the four-masted barque *Lawhill*, of which Jarvis himself was Master.

The arrival of these larger ships designed for increased cargo capacity rather than speed, in the main heralded the end of fast passage-making. Even Captain Robson, who had the *Corunna* on her maiden voyage and commanded her for three years of her short career, never equalled the passages he made in the *Talavera*. None the less, the *Corunna*'s maiden voyage in 1893-1894 was creditable:

Plate 10   The Launch of the Hougomont, *1897.*
Captain Hardie with white beard is on the left.
Mr. Russell is said to be the stout gentleman on the right in top hat.
From Mrs. Ethel Hardie's papers

Glasgow	to	Rio de Janeiro	40 days
Rio de Janeiro	to	Melbourne	55 days
Melbourne	to	London	89 days

In September, 1898, under Captain McNeil, she sailed from Barry Docks loaded with coal for Japan, going south about round Australia. This was a long haul of 17,500 miles which took 136 days. In 1901, she went out from Liverpool to Sydney in 94 days but followed this with a slow passage from Newcastle, N.S.W. to San Francisco of 89 days. In 1904, with a new Captain on board, she was unfortunately lost on the coast of Argentina, as we shall see later.

In 1895, J. Hardie & Co. once again moved to new premises in Glasgow, this time to 11, Bothwell Street. Although the Hardie family now held the reins, the bulk of the shares appear to have belonged to the Russell family, for example, the 64 shares of the *Nivelle, Hougomont* and *Archibald Russell* were apportioned as follows:

Nivelle	47/64	A. Russell
	17/64	J. Hardie
Hougomont	52/64	A. Russell
	12/64	J. Hardie
Archibald Russell	All shares held by James, John, Jackson and William Russell.	

During the next few years the firm suffered heavy losses, no less than four in ten years: the *Talavera*, which has already been mentioned, wrecked off Talcahuano in 1896; the *Pyrenees* lost in the Pacific in 1900; the *Saragossa* cast ashore on a remote South Sea Island in 1904; and the *Corunna* stranded on the Argentine coast the same year. However, the *Archibald Russell* was not a replacement; the last two losses took place months after the new ship was being considered.

Captain Robert Bryce commanded the *Pyrenees* from the time she left the builder's yard to the end of her short life under Hardies' houseflag. He started off her maiden voyage with a smart passage of 86 days from Glasgow to Sydney, followed by 39 days from Newcastle, N.S.W. to Valparaiso with a cargo of coal and 43 days in ballast from Callao back to Newcastle. The next leg of the voyage took her to Bassein in Burma. This occupied 58 days to Diamond Island at the entrance to the River Chindwin. Her homeward passage to Queenstown was a lengthy one taking 143 days, not up to Captain Bryce's usual standard, but perhaps by this time, the Pyrenees's bottom may have been foul. She arrived in Bremerhaven on September 20th, 1893, to discharge. In 1894 she loaded timber at Fredrikstadt and sailed out to Melbourne in 104 days. That year, the *Cutty Sark* made her last homeward wool passage in 86 days.[1] By comparison, the *Pyrenees* came home from Melbourne in 95 to London. She then crossed the Atlantic to New York and embarked on two consecutive voyages with case-oil to the Far East.

On the second case-oil voyage which was to Japan, she was 96 days to Anjer. After discharging the cargo at Nagasaki, she ran across the Pacific to Puget Sound in 36 days, nearly matching the four-masted barque *Queen Margaret*, a noted flyer, which also sailed from Nagasaki and made the crossing to 'Frisco in 32. Both ships were matched again on the homeward leg: the *Queen Margaret* sailed from San Francisco on November 21st, while the *Pyrenees* sailed from Tacoma on November 23rd. Both ships arrived at Queenstown on March 12th, 1897, the *Queen Margaret* 111 days out and the *Pyrenees*, having sailed the longer distance, making her passage in 109.[2] Her remaining voyages continued better than average:

1897	Hamburg	to	Sydney	97 days
1898	Newcastle N.S.W.	to	'Frisco	52 days
1898	'Frisco	to	Falmouth	120 days
1898	Liverpool	to	Sydney	86 days
1898	Newcastle N.S.W.	to	'Frisco	72 days
1899	'Frisco	to	Dublin	136 days

The next voyage of the *Pyrenees* was the last for J. Hardie & Co. Captain Bryce sailed her in 26 days from Dublin to New York where she loaded case-oil for Shanghai. This time she was 88 days to Anjer, reaching Shanghai 33 days later. The next passage across the Pacific to Port Townsend started off very slowly and it took Captain Bryce 23 days to work her over the first 1,500 miles. One may wonder why the *Pyrenees* was so long in covering this comparatively short distance; light southerly winds and the north-going Kuro Siwo current may have hampered him in weathering the southern tip of Honshu; but anyway, the *Pyrenees* was off Yokohama on August 17th, when she got the wind she wanted and romped

Plate 11 No 11, Bothwell Street. Hardies' old office was the corner apartment and is now a 'sandwich supermarket' as the sign shows.
P. Strathdee

across the Pacific in 22 days, averaging just under eight knots all the way.

The loss of the *Pyrenees* in 1900 makes interesting reading, a romantic saga of the days of sail and an example of the hazards facing the crews of the ships and the pitfalls of shipowning. It occurred on an island in the Pacific Ocean so remote that the news of the loss did not reach the office in Bothwell Street until some time had elapsed after the event. In the dark, dreary days of December just before Christmas, the information came that the *Pyrenees* was ashore on the island of Mangareva.

Mangareva? The name probably caused some head-scratching as to where it was. As far as the office knew, the *Pyrenees* had left Tacoma on October 14th with a cargo of wheat and barley, destined for Leith, and normally at this time they would have been expecting her to be approaching Cape Horn.

It was some time later before they learned the full story. A fortnight after the *Pyrenees* left Tacoma, the cargo was found to be on fire. Some of the wheat was said to have been loaded in a damp condition and it was presumed that the fire was started by spontaneous combustion and was so deep in the hold that it was impossible to reach. The only recourse was to lay the ship on some sheltered sandbank in order that the hold could be flooded. But where to do this was the problem which confronted the Master. The mainland was some 3,000 miles to windward, while to leeward lay thousands of tiny islands, a vast archipelago bestrewn with treacherous reefs. Captain Bryce decided to steer for Pitcairn Island where some sort of assistance might be available, or if not, at least the crew could be landed in safety. Sailing ships from North American ports took their course westward, using the trade winds to carry them south to the latitudes where the Roaring Forties would drive them round the Horn. This wandering course brought the Pitcairn Islanders one of their few contacts with the outside world and on December 2nd, when the *Pyrenees* hove into sight, they went out as they always did in their boats to greet her.

The Captain learned from the Governor of the island, a man named McCoy, a descendant of the *Bounty* mutineers, that there was no suitable place on Pitcairn Island where it would be possible to beach the *Pyrenees*, but that 300 miles to leeward was the island of Mangareva with sandy beaches where a ship could take the ground and lie. McCoy was prepared to pilot the ship there. Captain Bryce agreed to this and the ship's head was turned north-east and the yards squared for a quick run.

When it was most needed, the wind fell light and the comparatively short distance was covered at an agonisingly slow speed, while the fire

Plate 12   The Pyrenees *as the* Manga Reva *under the American flag*
A.D. *Edwardes Collection, State Library of South Australia*

raged down below and the decks became unbearably hot. The approach to
Mangareva from the south-east is clear of reefs which lie to the north.
None the less, the ship had to be conned through a maze of islets and
rocks, but this was accomplished with the help of McCoy and somewhere
on that small, green, palm-covered island, in some long-forgotten corner,
the *Pyrenees* was finally beached.

It appears that the fire had done too much damage for the ship to be
worth salvaging. The crew were taken to Tahiti by schooner and eventually reached home to sail again another day. The underwriters paid out the
claim for the ship and cargo and as far as J. Hardie & Co. were concerned
the matter was ended. But in actual fact, the hulk was examined by two
American Master Mariners and, deciding that she was not too badly damaged, they purchased her and set about patching her up. When fully
restored she was renamed *Manga Reva* and sailed for many years under
the American flag.[3]

Chapter IV

The Keel is Laid

In April, 1904, shortly after the death of Mr Russell, in pursuance of their plan to build a ship and name her after him, Hardies engaged in negotiating a price with Scotts. It was a good time to purchase: the depressed state of shipping and shipbuilding gave Hardies a chance to drive a hard bargain and the correspondence shows their efforts in this direction.[1] The previous sailing ship built for them by Scotts was the *Saragossa* in 1902, a vessel similar in size and rig to the new one they required. The price at that time was £22,700 but since then both the cost of materials and the wages of shipyard workers had fallen and they hoped to get a worthwhile reduction. The new ship was to be a duplicate of the *Hougomont* built for them in 1897 and they estimated that they could save £800 by having pitch pine decks instead of yellow pine, £250 by cutting down on sails and a further £100 on cheaper paint and anchor cables. Accordingly, in reply to Scotts' estimate of £22,500, Hardies suggested that £20,500 for the completed ship would be reasonable.

The offer was too low for Scotts to accept and they held out for a further £250. Hardies agreed to this. They had driven a hard bargain and £20,750 was going to leave the builders very little profit. Hardies, in their turn, were a little concerned as to whether they had skimped too much, especially over the pitch pine decks, and urged Scotts to make sure the timber was purchased in good time and given a chance to season properly.

Scotts undertook to commence building right away and informed Hardies that the ship, which now had the yard number 391, should be completed in about seven months. By May 19th, all was agreed and in a letter to the shipbuilders Hardies stated that they would like the launch to take place in early January in order, as they put it, 'that the vessel would be a 1905 ship'.

In November, Scotts were asked to fit a wheelhouse at the after end of the poop. In the specifications it was referred to as a 'hood', which would cover the steering mechanism and give the helmsman a certain amount of shelter. It covered an area of 10 ft by 10 ft and was 7 ft 5 ins at the highest point at the forward end where the helmsman stood. It was constructed of quarter inch steel and cost £37, which was a very modest sum.

A further expense which entailed some considerable correspondence

Plate 13   The Archibald Russell *on the stocks*
Scotts' Shipbuilding Co. Ltd.

was concerned with the bilge keels. These were fitted to steamers as a matter of course in order to reduce rolling in a seaway, but it was rare for a sailing ship to have them. However, it was Hardies' opinion that anything which might minimise the rolling in the new ship would reduce wear and tear on the rigging and in the long run save expense. The proposed bilge keels consisted of 6 in x 4 in 'T' bars riveted to the plates at the turn of each bilge for a length of 120 ft. To this was riveted a 9 in x $\frac{1}{2}$ in strip of steel plate with a bulb along the outer edge for strength. The cost estimated by Scotts was between £120 and £130. However, before laying out this amount of money, Hardies decided to seek further advice.

The firm of George Duncan & Co. of London owned a four-masted barque called the *Colonial Empire*, which had been experimentally fitted with bilge keels and an enquiry to them was favoured by a letter on November 15th, stating that they regarded the experiment as having been a success. They suggested that if Hardies wished further confirmation, the Master of the *Colonial Empire*, Captain David Watson, was available for interview. Captain Fullerton, who was superintending the building of No. 391, met Captain Watson who came out strongly in favour of bilge keels.

Hardies, still feeling that they needed to be convinced before laying out

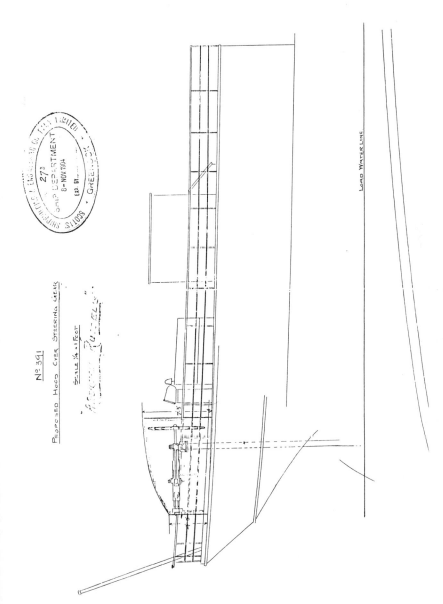

Fig 1 Proposed hood over steering gear

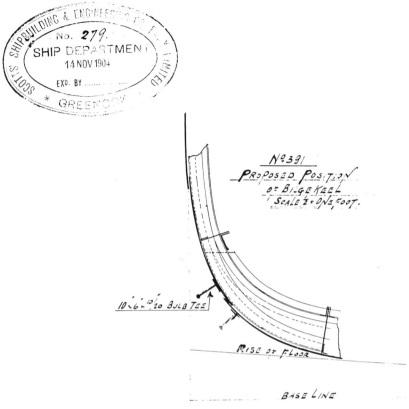

SHIPBUILDING & ENGINEERING CO LIMITED
No. 279.
SHIP DEPARTMENT
14 NOV 1904
EXD. BY ....
* GREENOCK

Nº 391
PROPOSED POSITION
OF BILGE KEEL
SCALE ½ = ONE FOOT.

10' 6" - 10' 20 BULB TEE

RISE OF FLOOR

BASE LINE

Fig 2 Plan of position of bilge keels

additional capital, contacted an eminent naval architect, Mr A. Mylne of Glasgow, and submitted a plan. In his reply, Mr Mylne did not seem to concern himself with reduction in rolling, for he never mentioned it in his letter, but he did state that it was his belief that the keels would be 'of material assistance to windward work under sail'.[2]

The cost of the sails was more than expected in spite of a certain amount of scrimping. The sailmakers George Rose & Sons made one complete suit for each mast including staysails. Of spare sails there were enough for one mast only, i.e. one spare foresail, one upper and one lower topsail, one upper and one lower topgallant and one spare royal. There was also one spare inner jib and a spare foretopmast staysail. However, if this appears a bit meagre, when the *Archibald Russell* set sail on her maiden voyage, she had a sailmaker on board who would spend most of his time stitching sails, building up a set of spares and repairing the worn ones. It was far cheaper than having them made in a sail loft.

The cost of the original set of sails, together with boat covers, mast covers, hatch tarpaulins, skylight covers, windsails and awnings came to £694.15s.5d, instead of the £600 budgeted for, but eventually a price of £655 seems to have been accepted. This was probably very reasonable. At the end of her career in 1939, a complete suit of sails for the *Archibald Russell* would have cost in the region of £3,000.

While the negotiations over the building of 391 were going on, the *Saragossa*, on passage from Newcastle, N.S.W. to San Francisco, was cast away on the island of Mangaia in the middle of the Pacific Ocean. Her first voyage, from which she never returned, had been a lengthy one.

In all, Hardies only had her nineteen months before she was lost and because of her short career, during which misfortune and lengthy passages appeared to have been her lot, she must be deemed to have been an unlucky ship. At her launch, she failed to slide down the ways at the appointed time, and on her maiden voyage, the run round to the loading port was not without incident. On this occasion, she sailed in ballast from Dundee on October 29th, 1902, for Liverpool, where she was chartered to load a general cargo. Gales and contrary winds forced her to run for shelter, first to Long Hope in the Isle of Hoy, not far from Scapa Flow, where she remained at anchor for three whole weeks.

Her Master at this time and for the first part of the maiden voyage was Captain Steven, who had recently left the *Vimeira* to take command; he did not seem to have employed a tug on the run round to Liverpool—at least there is no mention of one in Hardies' Movement Book—and this must account for the unusually long passage. Anyway, having found a safe anchorage at Long Hope on October 31st, Captain Steven required a favourable wind to permit her to leave, but for the next three weeks, according to the weather records, the *Saragossa* was beset by either westerly winds against which she could make no headway, or south-easterly ones which kept her pinned down at her anchorage. It was not until November 20th that an east wind enabled her to weigh and proceed. After this, she had a good run through the Pentland Firth, round Cape Wrath, down the North Minch into the Little Minch where Captain Steven was forced to shelter in Loch Snizort in the north of the Isle of Skye on November 22nd.

South-easterly gales kept the *Saragossa* there for a week, but on November 30th, she was able to make Loch Bracadale. Two days later she reached Tobermory, where again she was held up by south-easterly gales and it was not until December 6th that she was able to resume her protracted journey. She finally reached Liverpool on December 10th, having taken 42 days to cover 622 miles.

Plate 14 After the launch
Scotts' Shipbuilding Co. Ltd.

After loading, the *Saragossa* sailed from Liverpool on January 8th, 1903. She was 'spoken' just south of the Line, on the 37th day, finally arriving at Sydney on May 6th, 115 days out. After discharging, she did a round voyage from Newcastle, N.S.W. to San Francisco with coal, then lumber back to Port Pirie. Captain Steven left in 'Frisco, his place being taken by Captain Duncan, and under his command she soon after sailed to her fate. From Port Pirie she went to Newcastle, N.S.W. again for another coal cargo destined for 'Frisco. She left Newcastle on July 26th, but never arrived. The date of the stranding is recorded as August 15th, 1904, but it is doubtful whether Hardies heard about it until some weeks or months after, as Mangaia Island, one of the Cook Group, was so remote that according to one source it was a year before the crew were rescued.

At some point on the wandering route which the *Saragossa* followed, she had to pass through numerous atolls and reefs, some of them not properly charted, and almost all completely unlighted at that time. As she approached the Cook Islands on that fateful evening, Captain Duncan did not realise that the ship was 20 miles further north than his reckoning. As darkness fell, the chance of seeing the low-lying islands in time to take avoiding action was slender and by the time the chilling cry 'breakers

34

ahead' was shouted from the fo'c'sle head, her fate was sealed. One can imagine the situation with the scene lit by tropic starlight; the trade winds driving the ship steadily towards the reef, sails shaking and booming, blocks clattering as the crew attempted to bring the ship to the wind in an effort to beat their way out of danger. No time to clear the anchors stowed and lashed down on the fo'c'sle head after leaving Newcastle for the long passage. Close to leeward is the white surf watched anxiously by all. Then she strikes with a rending of steel as she plunges across the reef, her bottom torn, masts and yards crashing down with the sudden impact.

With the help of the islanders, mainly Polynesians, all except two of the crew managed to get through the surf to the shore by means of a lifeline. The unfortunate two who didn't make it drowned in the attempt and were later buried ashore. For the *Saragossa* it was the end, but for the crew it was the beginning of a long exile. The ship was systematically pillaged by the natives, but what stores survived helped to augment the fish and taro which were to be their diet in the long months as castaways before the New Zealand authorities, over 2,000 miles away, sent help. Communications were mostly by island schooner, which accounts for the time lapse before they were finally rescued.[3]

Before the month was out, the firm suffered another loss. This time it was the *Corunna*, stranded near the River Plate when on passage from Antwerp to Port Townsend with a cargo of cement. It was an unfortunate loss which might have been avoided. James Hardie thought very highly of the *Corunna* and wrote about her in *Sea Breezes* in 1927:

> She was a wonderful ship in many ways, as notwithstanding her big carrying, she turned out to be marvellously fast, and a magnificent sea boat. 'Frisco to Falmouth in 124 days. Vessel partially dismasted north of the Equator on this trip, and arrived at Falmouth under jury rig.

He continues with a remark on her speed during a voyage from Philadelphia to Hiogo:

> On this voyage she logged in one week 1,982 miles which gives an average speed of 11.8 knots. This occurred in 45 and 46 latitudes, running her easting down.

It will be remembered that Captain Robson had the *Corunna* from the stocks and it was he who got the most out of her in her early days. He was followed by Captain McNeil, but on her last voyage there had been a change of Masters and the new man's name was John Mason. He had previously been Captain of the full-rigged ship *Albuera* which he left in May, 1904, to join the *Corunna* in Antwerp the following June. His one and only voyage in the *Corunna* started badly. She left Antwerp for Port Townsend in the State of Washington on July 24th, 1904, passing Flushing soon after midnight on the 25th, with a tug towing ahead and a pilot in charge. The weather was unsettled and the tug was unable to maintain sufficient speed in the squalls, and during one particularly heavy one just as they were passing the Wandelaar Light Vessel the pilot, through an error of judgement as the Captain stated in his report afterwards, gave the order to cast off the tow rope, with the result that the *Corunna*, with insufficient steerage way, drifted down on the light vessel and collided with her. Fortunately the damage was confined to dents and a few broken stanchions, but the *Corunna* put back to Flushing Roads.

On the 27th, she set sail again and, after a slow time of 66 days, at 6.00 pm on August 30th, she was off Cape Corrientes, which showed up 11 miles on the lee beam according to Captain Mason's estimate. She was close hauled on the port tack, making a course of south-west in a strong gale with hard squalls. Either the *Corunna* was making more leeway than Captain Mason calculated or he was a great deal closer to the land than he expected, because at 11.00 pm, the shore suddenly loomed up less than a mile off, both ahead and on the lee beam. All hands were called and the order given to wear ship and they were in the process of doing this when, with the yards squared and the ship before the wind, she struck and bumped heavily on the sand. The seas started to break over her and when they sounded the well, they found she was making water fast.

The sea was too heavy to launch the boats and for over 24 hours the crew were unable to make any contact with the shore. When on 1st September people appeared on the beach, some of the crew threw their belongings into the sea and followed after them, and one of the seamen was drowned in spite of all efforts to save him. On the 2nd, the wind died away to a dead calm and the crew were taken aboard the tug *Malvenas*.

As far as J. Hardie & Co. were concerned, this was the end of the *Corunna*. She was abandoned to the underwriters and, although she was salvaged, she was no longer seaworthy and was relegated to a coal hulk. The Court of Inquiry at Buenos Aires was of the opinion that the Master was to blame for not taking more soundings and the current setting on shore had not been taken into account sufficiently.

*   *   *   *   *   *   *

At the time of the *Archibald Russell*'s building, the majority of shipowners had turned over to steam, realising that the sailing ship could no longer cope with the ever-increasing demand of the industrial nations for raw materials in their factories, and cereal to feed an expanding population. Her pace was too slow. To overcome this, the charterer offered much higher freights for steam tonnage, and since the steamship was often larger and could complete two or perhaps three voyages to a sailing ship's one, the annual profit might be counted in thousands of pounds, while those of the sailer were to be reckoned only in hundreds.

However, to return to the *Archibald Russell*. The Hardie brothers and their associates of the Russell family still preferred the adventure and charisma of the sailing ship. Their new ship was the last of a long line, built in the traditional way by Scottish craftsmen. She was a final fling, almost an act of indulgence. She marked the beginning of the end of shipowning in the old established, leisurely way.

*   *   *   *   *   *   *

The *Archibald Russell* was launched without masts, with only the bowsprit in place. Hardly any bunting served to brighten the dull winter's day save three flags, the Pilot Jack forward, the blue and white flag of Hardies' fleet above the donkey house and the Red Ensign aft. A paddle steamer attended her in the stream and towed her to the Cartsburn Graving Dock, where the masts were to be stepped and the rigging and painting completed.

Chapter V

The Ship

According to the records, the *Archibald Russell* sailed from Greenock on February 28th, 1905, fully rigged and ready in all respects for the run to the loading port, five weeks to the day since she was launched. Such a short period to convert a hulk to complete rig seems quite an achievement. The finished article was a fine-looking vessel of 2,385 gross registered tonnage, designed to carry a cargo of 3,800 tons on a mean draught of 21 ft 7½ ins. Her measurements were 291 ft 5 ins length with a moulded beam of 43 ft 2½ ins. Her forecastle was 36 ft long and her poop measured 54 ft from the break to the end of her counter stern.

There is nothing finer than a brand new ship when she is handed over to her owner straight from the shipyard; every part of her clean, the new paint and varnish work fresh and shining. A visitor stepping aboard on that day, viewing the ship in all the glory of her newness, would note the orderliness of everything: yards squared, ropes neatly coiled, everything shipshape and Bristol fashion, altogether a ship staunch in hull and well found aloft.

New she may have been, but even for a sailing ship, her owners had not moved with the times by incorporating in the design technical improvements already successful in other sailing ships, which would have made her more economical to run. The increase in the capital cost may have been a consideration, or an innate conservatism on the part of J. Hardie & Co. Scotts, who had been building ships since 1840 and are reputed to have built the first clipper, had produced a fine ship in the *Archibald Russell*, but they were building to a price. Hardies do not seem to have considered installing ballast tanks which had been built into other sailing ships with great success and made considerable savings, since the usual way of ballasting was to purchase and load sand, shingle or building rubble, all of which had to be acquired at some cost and had to be discharged at the end of the voyage and disposed of in some way. Another improvement which might have been considered, one which was quite a common feature in large sailing ships, was the raised midship section or centrecastle which gave greater strength and was approved of by the underwriters who gave reduced insurance premiums to ships designed in this fashion.

In other ways the fingers of utility, or perhaps parsimony, had touched the *Archibald Russell*. There were few of the decorations so dear to

Plate 15 View of the poop
R. Rasmussen

shipowner and seaman alike in the 19th century. Teakwood deckhouses had given way to steel, carvings and scrollwork had been dispensed with and a fiddlehead had taken the place of a figurehead. Bare, uncluttered and workmanlike decks were the features of the *Archibald Russell*.

The poop, under which the Master and officers lived, was the seat of authority. From the forward end, the Mate on watch could view the maindeck and at the same time keep his eye on the weather side of the sails. By means of the catwalk which bridged the spaces between the poop and the fo'c'sle head, he could quickly reach the scene of any activity without going down on the maindeck. At the after end of the poop was the wheelhouse, open at the fore end; this structure, apart from keeping the helmsman dry, reduced the danger to him resulting from the ship being pooped by a heavy sea. Both wheel and helmsman could be casualties on such occasions, the loss of steering sometimes being fatal to the ship. The wheel was of teak, 5 ft in diameter and brass bound. The steering compass stood just before the wheel and forward of this the saloon skylight, and then the chartroom which also gave access by a stairway to the accommodation below. The standard compass, by which the course was set and bearings taken, was situated on an extension of the poop, giving as clear a view as was available and as far from the magnetic disturbance as possible. The teak rails at the fore end of the poop were supported by nicely turned wooden stanchions.

A door from the quarterdeck led into the port alleyway of the poop where the officers were accommodated. The cabins of the two Mates and the steward were on the right, and on the left was the messroom. Then came the stairway to the chartroom, with the door to the saloon at the after end. The saloon was the Captain's domain, tastefully panelled out in fine wood with plush red upholstered furnishings, rather like a room in a Victorian club. His cabin led off the starboard side as did the bathroom and toilet, and on the port side were cabins for passengers or pilot. A table with swivel chairs round it stood in the centre of the saloon. In the daytime, light filtered adequately through the skylight while at night, the place was lit by a brass lantern swinging free on a hook above the table.

On the starboard side of the poop was the sailroom, one of the driest places on board and easily aired by opening the starboard door to the quarter deck. Here work on the sails, old and new, was carried out. Below this was the sail locker, entered by a trapdoor, where spare sails were kept. Beneath the pantry was a lazarette, entered by a similar trapdoor, where all the food for the voyage was stored. The Mates' washplace was to port and the lavatory to starboard, both outside the accommodation as if as an

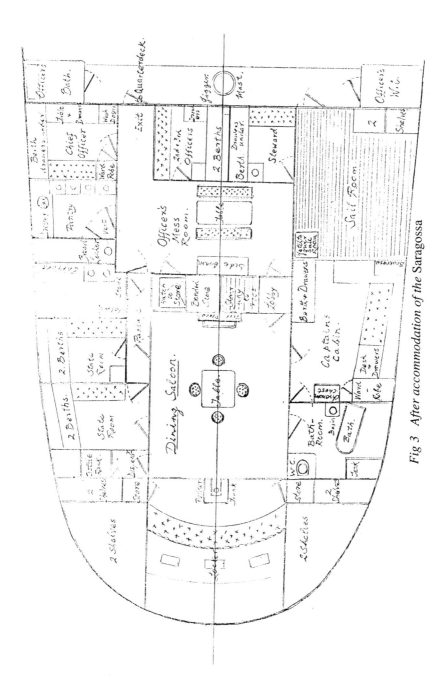

Fig 3 After accommodation of the Saragossa

41

afterthought, or not considered suitable offices to include within the living quarters. They were entered from the quarterdeck. In general, the layout was similar to that of the *Saragossa*, a blueprint of which survives in the Strathclyde Archives.

Teak ladders on either side of the poop led down to the quarterdeck where the full length of the maindeck could be seen rising with a beautiful sweep towards the fo'c'sle. There were three steel deckhouses situated between the masts: the seamen's house, the largest one, lay between the fore and main masts; the midship house between the main and mizzen. The latter contained the donkey boiler and machinery at the after end, while the galley occupied the fore end. The after deckhouse, known as the half-deck, lay abaft the mizzen and was the home of the apprentices and petty officers. None of the accommodation gave more than the barest comfort to the occupants but it was considered adequate at the time. In heavy weather the seas washed against the bulkheads and flooded out the rooms.

The main deck had openings for three hatches: the fore hatch and after hatch each 12 ft x 10 ft, and the main hatch 20 ft x 12 ft, all three with coamings 2 ft high. They were small by modern standards and, with the low freeboard of a sailing ship, extremely vulnerable during heavy weather. They were covered with wooden hatchboards and kept watertight by tarpaulins secured with battens and wedges. To protect them further, heavy baulks of timber were laid across and lashed down with ropes or wires to ring bolts. Then only were the hatches considered safe from being stove in.

At the fore end of the main deck, ladders led up to the topgallant fo'c'sle, more commonly known as the fo'c'sle head. Compared to the poop this was a bare, cheerless place. Here, the lookout spent his lonely vigil with no shelter from the weather. There was little chance of his falling asleep in the colder latitudes, the draught from the foresail and the driving spray making the watch a cold one. The light towers at the after end shielded the green and red sidelights. The crane at the fore-end was used for lifting the anchors inboard from where they were lashed securely on either side of the fo'c'sle when at sea. The capstan, the taskmaster of many weary hours of labour, stood in a central position directly above the windlass. A small hatch under the crane permitted gear to be hoisted from the store below. The fo'c'sle head was fitted with steel rails on both sides and at the after end there were teak hand rails supported by turned stanchions with the ship's bell mounted centrally.

The windlass was situated under the fo'c'sle head. It was connected by a clutch to the capstan above, which supplied the motive power when the donkey boiler was not in use. On the port side of the fo'c'sle were store

Plate 16 Archibald Russell *rigging view*
National Maritime Museum

rooms for paints, ropes, etc., and on the starboard side were the lavatories and washplace for the seamen. At the forward end, almost up in the eyes, were the cable stoppers and a hatch down into the forepeak below.

The *Archibald Russell* was equipped with four boats, two of which were in skids on either side of the standard compass platform, launched by means of radial davits. The other two boats were stowed on skids beside the midship house. They might be termed long boats, having transom sterns and being narrower and longer than the double-ended wooden lifeboats which were becoming more popular. When they were required to be launched, tackles had to be rigged from the mainyard and these boats could not be launched quickly in an emergency.

Since the *Archibald Russell* was one of the last sailing vessels to be built in the United Kingdom, it is surprising that she was not given more

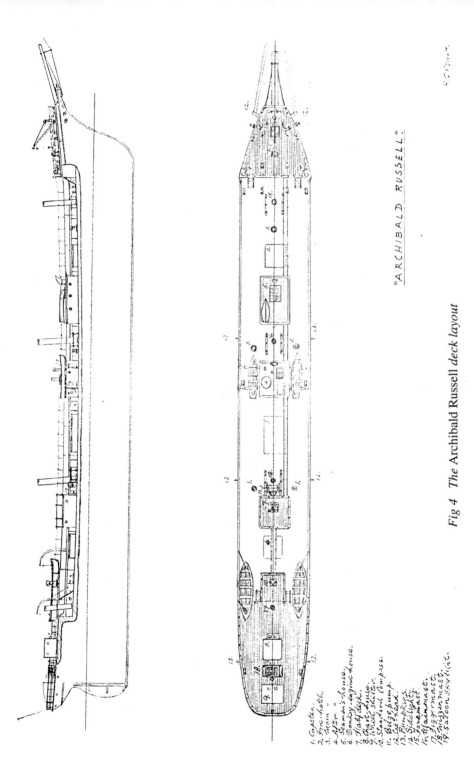

"ARCHIBALD RUSSELL"

Fig 4   The Archibald Russell deck layout

1. Capstan.
2. Forecastle.
3. Fore "
4. After "
5. Seamen's house.
6. Donkey-engine house.
7. Half deck.
8. Chart house.
9. Wheel shelter.
10. Standard Compass.
11. Bilge pump.
12. Cat head.
13. Pumpbrakes.
14. Sidelights.
15. Fore mast.
16. Mainmast.
17. Jiggermast.
18. Mizzenmast.
19. Saloon skylight.

44

Plate 17   Starboard side looking aft
Sea Breezes Archives

45

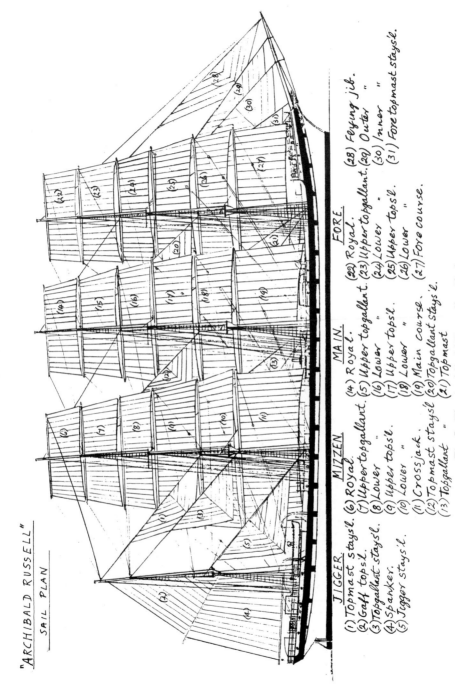

"ARCHIBALD RUSSELL"
SAIL PLAN

JIGGER.
(1) Topmast stays'l.
(2) Gaff tops'l.
(3) Topgallant stays'l.
(4) Spanker.
(5) Jigger stays'l.

MIZZEN
(6) Royal.
(7) Upper topgallant.
(8) Lower "
(9) Upper tops'l.
(10) Lower "
(11) Crossjack.
(12) Topmast stays'l
(13) Topgallant "

MAIN.
(14) Royal.
(15) Upper topgallant.
(16) Lower "
(17) Upper tops'l.
(18) Lower "
(19) Main course.
(20) Topgallant stays'l.
(21) Topmast "

FORE.
(22) Royal.
(23) Upper topgallant.
(24) Lower "
(25) Upper tops'l.
(26) Lower "
(27) Fore course.
(28) Flying jib.
(29) Outer "
(30) Inner "
(31) Fore topmast stays'l.

Fig 5   The Archibald Russell sail plan

46

labour-saving devices such as brace and halliard winches which had already been considered for the *Saragossa*, not so much for the ease and comfort of the mariner but in order to reduce the number of crew required. It is true that she had the donkey boiler and engine, and use of this could be made by connecting it to the windlass by means of an endless chain known as a 'messenger'. Also the yards could be hoisted when making sail, but steam was rarely used at sea for the sake of economy. The donkey engine was primarily for the loading and discharging of cargo in places where there were no other facilities. Considering the ship had three hatches, a winch at each one would have made cargo work easier and quicker. With only one steam winch, it would have been difficult although not impossible to work more than one hatch at a time. When under Hardies' flag, hand-operated winches known as 'dolly winches' were used in the fore and after hatches for hoisting out or loading cargo.

There was a hand pump at the after end of the fo'c'sle which could be used for washing down the decks. This was connected to a pipe which led along the starboard topgallant rail with three hydrants. If a hose had ever been supplied it disappeared after a few years and was never replaced. This pump was used to fill the donkey boiler by buckets from the nearest available hydrant. It was the accepted thing to use salt water.

She was well equipped with capstans. Apart from the one on the fo'c'sle head there were five others strategically sited around the deck for general use. There was one abaft the foremast, one on each side of the main and two more at the mizzen. There were capstan bars in racks nearby and, although powered by muscle, these capstans were invaluable for hoisting the yards or sheeting home the sails or any other jobs where extra purchase was required.

To empty the well there was a manually operated pump placed abaft the mizzen mast between the fife-rails. This machine, with its large flywheel and curved spokes, operated twin suctions and was the only means of clearing the ship of water. It would have been of great practical advantage if it had been possible to connect this pump to the donkey engine, but it did not seem to have been thought necessary to do this. There is no record that it was ever used except for pumping out seepage from cargoes or rainwater.

As with Hardies' other ships, the *Archibald Russell* was given a generous sail plan at a time when all shipowners were attempting in various ways to save money with reduced sail area. Her rig was considered rather square by some, but the proportions gave her an advantage in looks over those vessels which carried no royals and were in consequence unkindly

Plate 18 The Archibald Russell *towing away from the Clyde for Port Talbot*
Scotts' Shipbuilding Co. Ltd.

referred to by seamen as 'baldheaded'. With double topsails and topgallants, she was like a hundred other four-masted barques. Her mainmast stood 169 ft from waterline to truck. The mainyard was 90 ft and the main royal 50 ft. The yards were interchangeable between the fore, main and mizzen, each spar being the same size as its counterpart on the other two masts. The fore, main and mizzen masts were in three sections and well stayed with double capstays on the lower masts and single topmast capstays. It was quite common at this time to make the lowermast and topmast in one long pole, but this was not favoured by some Scottish shipyards and her topmasts and topgallantmasts were fidded in the usual way. She was strongly rigged, built for driving in gale force winds and throughout her life she suffered only minor damage to her gear. Her sail area was 33,000 square ft.

Her colour scheme was pleasing to the eye. The line of black gunports against a white painted background gave her a graceful appearance exceeding that of ships without these decorations. The bulwarks were black and the topsides below the black painted moulding at the base of the sheerstrake were grey, contrasting vividly with the red boot topping. The deckhouses and inside of the bulwarks were painted brilliant white. The masts and yards were pale brown, a paint used on the spars of so many ships because of its durability and commonly known among seamen as 'mast colour'.

Such a ship was the *Archibald Russell*. She would, by modern standards, be considered small with living quarters poky, dark and comfortless, especially with regard to the crew. But there were worse ships around, meaner, less comfortable and more demanding in some ways. Times were hard, the pay was low, but to many seamen sail was still the life they preferred. She was a ship in which men were proud to sail and although she was not expected to be a flyer, she always had the reputation of being a smart ship which could hold her own with the best.

On February 28th, 1905, she left the Clyde under tow for Port Talbot. She had not signed on her crew yet and was lightly ballasted with only the lower sails bent. Her yards were squared to a 'T' and her paint shone. She was smart, shipshape and ready to earn her living in the trade routes of the oceans, one of Kipling's 'shuttles in the loom of Empire'. Significantly, the Empire was to disappear soon after the demise of the sailing ship which opened up the oceans and made such an Empire possible.

Chapter VI

First Sailing

Since the Russell family's business was coal, it was to be expected that the *Archibald Russell*'s cargoes would involve her in that trade. At that time, and for many years after, coal was the mainstay of the export trade and the majority of tramps, whether sail or steam, carried it as a matter of course. It was exported to all four corners of the world for use on railways, as ships' bunkers and in other industries. A sailing ship might be chartered to load coal for Rio de Janeiro, Iquique or San Francisco. Other coal cargoes were carried to Singapore or further east to Chinese ports. Such cargoes had their problems. They took a long time to discharge, especially in the more remote ports where a ship had to use her own gear. Also, coal was subject to spontaneous combustion, and if improperly trimmed, liable to shift in heavy weather. In spite of this, it was always welcome as the alternative to an unprofitable outward passage in ballast.

So, for her first cargo, the *Archibald Russell* was chartered to load coal for Iquique. Where the next cargo was to come from depended on whether a nitrate cargo was offered homewards from Chile. If not, she might have to go to Australia for wheat, or California for barley, according to the season. Other possibilities were sugar from Hawaii, a cargo of guano from some remote island or a ballast passage across the Pacific for another cargo of coal from Newcastle, N.S.W., back to a Chilean port.

The tow to the loading port was completed in three days. Port Talbot at this time was a small place enjoying a large coal export trade. There was much to be done before the *Archibald Russell* was ready to sail on her first voyage. The ballast was discharged and she was shifted to the tips, where for days she lay under a pall of dust while the holds were filled with 3,800 tons of coal. When this was completed the crew were signed on, stores and water taken aboard and the upper sails bent.

The Captain on her maiden voyage was Charles Lowe, a rugged seaman of fifty-eight who came from Fife.[1] His previous ship was Hardies' *Hougomont*. He commanded her for a period of seven years which included a disastrous voyage in 1903 when she was driven ashore in the Solway Firth.[2] The Movement Book kept in Hardies' office and meticulously written up is quite terse about this episode:

February 22nd 1903	off Lynas Point
February 25th	in Maryport Roads
February 26th	left for Liverpool in tow of tug
February 27th	ashore at Allonby

As might be expected, there was a great deal more behind those few words. The *Hougomont* had arrived off Point Lynas on February 22nd after a passage of 136 days from San Francisco with a general cargo for Liverpool, but before she could reach the safety of the River Mersey she was caught in a severe gale. In open waters, large sailing vessels like the *Hougomont* could cope with any weather, but they needed plenty of sea-room to manoeuvre. In the confined waters of the Irish Sea, Captain Lowe had expected to engage the services of a tug to bring his ship into the Mersey, but none was available, and finding himself embayed between Anglesey and the Mull of Galloway, he ran for 100 miles north to the doubtful safety of Maryport Roads where he brought the *Hougomont* to anchor. The tug *Brilliant Star* was sent to find her, and on the 26th, the tow to Liverpool commenced, but in the wild weather which was raging the tow-rope parted and the *Hougomont* was driven helplessly before the storm up the Solway Firth until she went aground off Allonby. There she was pounded by heavy seas which brought down the fore-topgallant and the main royal masts and stove in the hatches. The adjacent coastline was strewn with the tinned products of California. She was in a bad way, high and dry at low water and almost derelict, but she was salvaged and survived to sail again for many years. Captain Lowe was cleared of any mismanagement and now, two years after, we find him in command of the *Archibald Russell*.

Captain Lowe was undoubtedly a seaman of great experience, having the confidence of the Hardie brothers as shown by the way they continued to employ him after the stranding of the *Hougomont*. He appears to have been an active man for his years; tough and resourceful but having a hot temper when roused.

On the *Archibald Russell*'s maiden voyage there were 32 men in the crew, including six apprentices. The Mate, William Johnstone, twenty-eight years old, came from the *Hougomont* as did the sailmaker, Duncan McRae*. The latter was fifty-two years old and having joined the

---

*It is doubtful if McRae knew his correct age. In 1905 he gave his age as 52, but two years later in 1907 his age was apparently 57. In 1912 it was 59, three years lost somewhere. In one set of articles his date of birth was given as 1850. He may have been 72 when he left the Archibald Russell in 1922.

Plate 19   The Archibald Russell
National Maritime Museum

Archibald Russell, stayed with her all her working life under the Red Ensign, leaving her at the age of sixty-nine when the ship was laid up and for sale. James Brown, twenty-two and William Irving, twenty-three, were Second and Third Mates respectively, neither of them possessing certificates of competency, although no doubt they were excellent seamen. There was a shortage of qualified men at this time as so many of the younger ones with certificates were transferring to steamships. Irving came from the clipper *Yallaroi* owned by Alex Nicol & Co. of Aberdeen, whose ships included the well-known *Cimba*, the *Torridon* and the *Romanoff*. These ships were employed in the Australian wool trade, but Nicols were now selling their ships and going out of business. The crew of the *Archibald Russell*, of diverse nationalities, were largely sailing ship men and the articles showed their previous ships as the *Loch Lomond*, the *Loch Torridon*, the *Thornliebank* and the *Forthbank* among other lesser known sailing ships. The Captain's wife, Eleanor, an Australian lady in her forty-eighth year, was signed on as purser with a nominal wage of one shilling per month.

The crew's wages ranged from £8 per month for the First Mate to 10/- for an ordinary seaman. The carpenter's wage, which was the highest of the petty officers at £5.10s per month, was greater than that of the Second Mate who only rated £5, while the Third Mate drew £3, the same as an able seaman, which shows that his services were not valued very highly since few sailing ships normally carried a Third Mate. The sailmaker was paid £5, the cook and the bosun £4.10s. The Captain's wages never appeared on the ship's articles, being a private agreement between himself and the owners.[3]

Such wages may well have been in advance of those paid ashore, but by no great margin, and in no way compensated for the hard work and danger which seamen were bound to encounter on a long, deep-sea voyage, but the shipowner considered the wages sufficient return for the period under articles; the crews were given a roof over their heads and were adequately fed, according to the Merchant Shipping Acts. For the rolling stone with no ties, poor though the wages were, the long voyage gave him little opportunity to spend them and the big pay-off at the end allowed him to go on a big spree before shipping out for another long spell at sea when his money ran out. One such rolling stone was a seaman called James Riley who joined on the last day in place of a seaman who had failed to turn up at sailing time. He was an unfortunate addition to the crew and caused much trouble later on.

They sailed for Port Talbot on March 21st. 28 days later, on April 18th, the *Archibald Russell* was south of the Cape Verde Islands in Latitude 9°N, Longitude 25°W, where she was spoken by the German steamship *La Plata*, outward bound to South America. Communication was made by flags of the International Code, the *Archibald Russell* identifying herself by hoisting her numbers followed by a request to be reported to Lloyds; since no ships were equipped with a wireless at this time, this had to wait until the German reached Santos where the Captain duly complied with the request.

The outward passage to Iquique took the *Archibald Russell* westward round Cape Horn. Her time on passage was 103 days, which was a comparatively slow one. The distance from Port Talbot to Iquique is 9,600 miles, which gave her an average speed of just under 4 knots, but sailing ships have to seek the winds most favourable to them, adding considerably to the total distance which a powered vessel might take over a more direct route. She was in the vicinity of Cape Horn in midwinter and the winter of 1905 was a particularly severe one in those waters with persistent westerly gales, during which half a dozen sailing ships were lost and a score or more driven to ports of refuge in distress.

She arrived at Iquique on July 2nd, and although her passage was not remarkable, Hardies must have been pleased with the news that she had arrived safely with no damage to ship or cargo, especially in view of all the casualties to other sailers. In comparison to her 103 day passage, the full-rigged ship *British Isles*, which sailed soon after the *Archibald Russell*, was 150 days to Pisagua, 39 miles up the coast to Iquique; she was badly battered by the weather off Cape Horn and was delayed several weeks effecting repairs. The previous year another full rigged ship, the *Brenda,* under Captain Learmont, who in his day was considered a competent shipmaster, made the same passage in 91 days.[4] Probably the best passages in 1905 were those of the French four-masted barque *Dunkerque* from Port Talbot and the German five-masted barque *Potosi* from the Lizard, which were both 67 days to Iquique.[5]

Plate 20 Iquique
National Maritime Museum

The coast of Chile was a desolate and dangerous region for sailing ships. Many of the ports were open roadsteads with deep water and poor holding ground. The Andes, towering 20,000 ft above, look down on this arid, treeless coastline where it never rains and the long Pacific rollers break upon the shore even in calm weather. Ashore, the cities were places of narrow streets, flies and shimmering heat. Tidal waves and earthquakes were not infrequent. Most vessels came with coal from Europe or Australia and sailed with copper, nitrate or guano. The port of Iquique was one such place. Ships arriving sailed into their berth without the aid of tugs, mooring among a host of other vessels lined up in tiers, with two anchors out forward and a kedge aft. It was common to see fifty vessels of all nationalities discharging or loading in this rather precarious harbour.

Making a landfall on this coast could be hazardous. Fickle winds caused vessels to drift with the current past their destination or even worse, to be set ashore and wrecked, having failed to find bottom with their anchors.

Such was the coast to which the *Archibald Russell* came. She joined the throng of ships and commenced discharging her coal into lighters. Moored in the tiers was the *Hougomont*, getting out the last part of the cargo which she had brought from Port Talbot. Also in Iquique, and in the same tier as the *Archibald Russell*, was the four-masted barque *Osborne* of Liverpool. One of her apprentices, J. Rogers, who crewed the Captain's gig, noted what a smart ship the *Archibald Russell* was, with everything brand spanking new. The Captain of the *Osborne* told the apprentices to call aboard the *Archibald Russell* and pick up a parcel for him, which they did, no doubt pleased to see fresh faces during the weeks of monotony. Their pleasure was somewhat dimmed when they found the parcel contained holystones,* of which the *Archibald Russell* had sufficient to spare and for which the boys gave scant thanks. However, they found that all was not well with the crew of the new ship.[6] Two men from the *Archibald Russell* had deserted and one died in hospital of typhoid fever. Captain Lowe saw fit to bring eleven seamen before the British Consul charged with various offences, and being guilty, they were eventually dismissed from the ship.[7]

The basis of the trouble which precipitated what became virtually a mutiny was the discharging of the coal cargo. On the west coast this was traditionally done by the crew and the seamen frankly resented it. In other ports of the world, cargoes were handled by organised stevedores, this being almost a necessity since sailors often went on drinking sprees. Anyway, they considered digging out coal beneath the dignity of a seaman whose job it was to hand, reef and steer. From the shipowner's point of view, using the crew to discharge the cargo was the cheapest method.

The thought of weeks of digging coal with no shore leave bred discontent among the crew of the *Archibald Russell* and they showed it by slowing down on the rate of discharge. Matters came to a head on July 13th when the Mate, Mr Johnstone, told them to get a move on with the job. All he got in return was a stream of abuse and he reported this to the Captain.

After dinner that day, Captain Lowe went to the main hatch to see if he could obtain any results. After speaking to the men he was told in no uncer-

---

*Holystones were sandstone blocks used for scouring wooden decks to whiteness, which seamen did on hands and knees, and were consequently known as 'bibles' or 'prayer books'. Holystoning was not a popular job.

tain terms that they did not give a damn for him and would work as fast as they pleased, and if he didn't like it, there was a good calaboose ashore which he could put them in for all they cared. The Captain entered the details in the official logbook, describing the language as vile and mutinous.

Not all the crew felt the same way, at least not to the extent of going to the calaboose, but all those who did, found a ready spokesman in James Riley, the pierhead jump, who joined at the last minute in Port Talbot. He was an able seaman of twenty-eight and hailed from Dublin. After work was over for the day, the Captain called him aft, deeming him to be the instigator of the trouble.

The proceedings started off formally with the Captain seated at the head of the table in the saloon. Riley stood in the middle and the First Mate at the doorway. When the Captain read the charge, Riley reacted violently. Knocking the Mate flying, he rushed from the saloon shouting to the crew to come aft and support him. The Captain and the officers went to the quarterdeck to be met by half the seamen advancing menacingly along the maindeck and it began to look as if a full-scale mutiny was brewing.

At first, Captain Lowe tried to get the crew to disperse, but a slanging match developed between him and Riley, who suddenly jumped at the Old Man, dealing him a heavy blow on the face with his fist. Then, before anyone could lay hold of him, he grabbed the Captain by the testicles and threw him to the deck. In spite of his fifty-eight years, Captain Lowe had plenty of fight in him and was quickly on his feet again and, driven by pain and fury, he had Riley by the throat and started throttling the life out of him. All hands gathered round and the two men were eventually separated. Considerably shaken, the Captain went to his cabin for his revolver, immediately returning on deck where he fired a shot in the air. He later stated that this was an accident, but whether or not, the deck was cleared. Meanwhile Riley made himself scarce. With revolver in hand and accompanied by his officers, Captain Lowe searched the ship for him without success. Later, the police were called aboard and Riley was winkled out from his hiding place and taken to gaol.

The following day a naval court was convened at the British Consulate, where Riley was found guilty of assaulting the Master and sentenced to twelve weeks in prison. Meanwhile, on board the *Archibald Russell*, twelve seamen refused duty when ordered to carry on with the discharge of the coal, and although the Consul came aboard to try and persuade them of the futility of their action, he was unable to make them change their minds. Next day, they were sent to prison for four weeks and the cost of substitutes to carry on the discharging was deducted from their wages.

Plate 21 Trade winds
C. Beneke

Peace returned to the *Archibald Russell* for four weeks until the seamen were sent back after completing their sentence. On August 15th, the day they returned, they once again refused duty and on the orders of the Consul they were put on bread and water. This provoked four of the more truculent seamen into acts of vandalism in which the fore and main topsail and topgallant halliards were cut, mooring ropes slashed and galley utensils thrown overboard. Although drink was never mentioned in the log, it would seem that the local *pisco* must have contributed to all the trouble.

The British Consul at Iquique by now was getting tired of the troubles of the *Archibald Russell*. Another Court of Inquiry had to be convened and sentences of a further four weeks, this time with hard labour, were given to those who refused duty, twelve weeks with hard labour for those who damaged the ship's gear and nine months for a seaman assaulting a shipmate.

Once more peace returned to the ship and the discharge of the cargo was resumed. Because of the trouble with the crew, it was a long job. Also there were many days when work was impossible due to bad weather in this exposed anchorage. The heavy swell caused the ships to roll and the barges ranged and bumped alongside, parting the moorings and causing them to seek the shelter of the mole until the weather moderated. Before all the cargo could be discharged, ballast was loaded, sufficient for good stability for her forthcoming voyage to Sydney.

Four months elapsed before all this was completed. The *Hougomont* had long since sailed and was loading a homeward cargo of grain in San Francisco and it was well on into November before the *Archibald Russell* was ready to sail. A motley lot of sailors of all nationalities was procured and signed on as able seamen, but Captain Lowe was forced to pay them £4.10s per month (£1.10s above the standard rate) and agree to discharge them at Sydney on arrival.

Getting away from the crowded anchorage was no easy matter. The result of miscalculation could be to drift alongside another vessel with probable damage to hull and rigging, or be cast ashore before the ship gained sufficient way to answer her helm. Crews from other ships came aboard and helped weigh the anchors and set the sails smartly. Usually the departure was effected smoothly with all the extra manpower and in this manner, on November 10th, 1905, the *Archibald Russell* started a leisurely voyage across the Pacific which occupied 90 days.

For a sailing ship and the hardworking windjammer seamen, this part of the ocean must have been one of the most pleasant. The greater part of the passage lies within the Tropic of Capricorn, where the South Equatorial Current flows steadily westward and the winds blow for the most part favourably and moderate. The ship's course for Iquique took her towards the Marquesas and passed northwards of these island paradises, their palm-fringed beaches beckoning the land-starved mariners. The Society Islands were left to port, the course trending southward, bringing the trade winds almost abeam. It was a lonely road across this vast ocean with ships rarely sighted. The Tropic of Capricorn was crossed south of New Caledonia and in this area strong winds were encountered as the Fiji Islands are the breeding grounds of hurricanes. It was January as she approached the Australian coast which is the season for these storms.

It is likely she had a good reception in Sydney. The arrival of a new and good-looking barque would raise a lot of interest around the waterfront. After a fine weather passage in ballast, she would be looking her best, especially around the decks. Her passage of 90 days however might not

Plate 22 Bowsprit view
C. Beneke

have raised any favourable comment, as there were vessels around at that time which could boast passages from Chilean ports of 60 days.

Little time was wasted in getting her ready for her homeward passage. She arrived on February 9th, 1906. Sixteen days later, on February 25th, with ballast discharged and the best part of 4,000 tons of wheat loaded, she slipped through Sydney Heads bound on the long road around Cape Horn to Falmouth.

The following day, the *Nivelle* sailed into Sydney Harbour, 74 days out from Port Townsend. The two ships may have sighted each other as they passed on their way, but they never met again as the *Nivelle* was wrecked shortly after. She was only nine years in the fleet before her loss and was noted rather for her lengthy passages than for speed. In 1898, she made a long one with case-oil from New York to Shanghai of 162 days, and two years later another equally lengthy one of 154 from New York to Hong Kong. However, there is no reason to believe she was not a good dividend earner and although comparisons might seem unfair, the four Masters who commanded her, Captains Williams, Steven, McMillan and Jones, all experienced men with long service with Hardies, never got as much out of her as Captain Bryce did out of her sister ship the *Pyrenees*. Captain Jones, who previously had the *Vimeira*, commanded the *Nivelle* on her last passage and ironically it was one of the best: 45 days from Newcastle, N.S.W. across the Pacific to a position a few miles off Antofagasta.

Meanwhile, the *Archibald Russell* was on her way to making the best homeward passage of her career from South Australia. She came round Cape Horn to the Line in 63 days where she was reported by the s/s *Corinthic* on April 29th; 30 days later on May 29th, she dropped anchor off Falmouth, 93 days from Sydney, the best passage of the season. Six other vessels arrived there on the same day, all of which had left Australia well before her, the next best passage being that of the full-rigged ship *Queen Elizabeth*, with 112 days from Sydney, while the poorest was that of the barque *Invermay* with 146.

Plate 23 The Nivelle
Scotts' Shipbuilding Co. Ltd.

The *Archibald Russell* lay there in company with these weatherbeaten vessels and during this time she received orders to proceed to Cardiff to discharge. On June 8th, the tug *Oceania* took her in tow and the following day she arrived in Cardiff, completing the round voyage from Port Talbot in just under fifteen months. She had, during this time, sailed 30,000 miles and delivered two cargoes.

Chapter VII

Second Voyage

While the *Archibald Russell* lay in Cardiff, the news reached Hardies' office that the *Nivelle* was ashore near Antofagasta and had become a total loss. The trouble occurred on June 30th, 1906, as she was nearing the end of a passage from Newcastle, N.S.W. She was approaching the anchorage when the wind fell right away, leaving her drifting at the mercy of the current which carried her steadily shorewards. Both anchors were dropped, but the depth of water was too great and they failed to hold. It was a situation from which there was no escape for the *Nivelle*. With no help at hand from a tug or passing steamer, and with her sails hanging limp and useless at the yards, she drifted until she touched the rocks upon which she was soon pounded to destruction.

1906 was the year that the Hardie brothers decided to try their hand with steamships. The first one was built at the yard of William Hamilton & Co., and was appropriately named *John Hardie*. The type of ship chosen by the brothers was the most popular with trampship owners, known as the 'three island steamer'. This type was so named because the forecastle, bridge and poop were raised above the level of the hull and when seen from a distance, almost 'hull down' as seamen say, appeared as three separate sections.

There was certainly nothing outstanding or glamorous about the s/s *John Hardie*, which was of 2,816 net tons and very much of a standard design and construction. She served the purpose for which she was intended quite adequately, namely the carriage of bulk cargoes for the most part, but if required, practically any commodity which could be manoeuvered through the hatch coamings. She was built of steel with a length of 375.4 ft, breadth 52.2 ft and a depth of hold 25.5 ft. Three coal fired boilers provided steam for her triple expansion engine giving a speed of 10 knots. She had five cargo hatches, 'tween decks and a deep tank in No 3 lower hold. Each mast had four derricks to deal with cargo, and sails were provided consisting of jib, staysail and trisail on the foremast and staysail and trisail on the main, but these were primarily used for steadying purposes. The accommodation for the officers was much about the same standard as in the Hardie sailing ships, adequate but rather poky, situated amidships. The sailors and firemen lived under the fo'c'sle head, the least comfortable part of the ship and a long way from the galley, which was placed in just about the worst situation possible between the funnel and engine-room. She

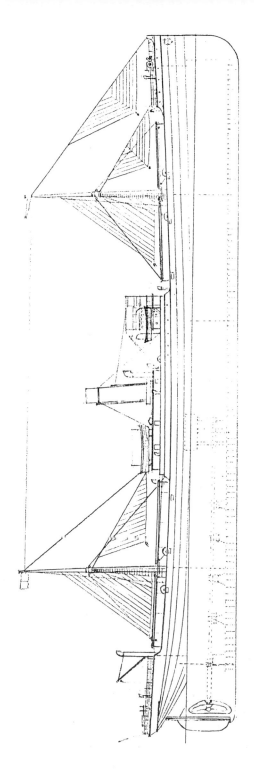

S.S. "JOHN HARDIE."

H.G. Hornby

Fig 6 s.s. John Hardie

63

could load 7,115 tons of wheat and spent some time in the River Plate trade, but she also traded much further afield as recorded in James Hardie's notebook which has survived the years and reveals jottings about voyages from the United States to South Africa with case-oil, and coal cargoes from Newcastle, N.S.W. to Manila, followed by calls at numerous ports in the Indonesian Archipelago on charter to one of the liner companies.

The *John Hardie* was well manned, far better than some other tramp steamers. Her crew consisted of 33 all told:

Captain	Chief Engineer
1st, 2nd & 3rd Mates	2nd, 3rd & 4th Engineers
Steward	1 Greaser
Cook	1 Donkeyman
Carpenter	9 Firemen
Boatswain	1 Mess Room Steward
7 Able Seamen	1 Firemen's Cook
1 Ordinary Seaman	

It was quite common to run a steamship of this size without a Third Mate or Fourth Engineer and moreover, the Second Mate was often expected to double as Boatswain with no extra pay, while as few as six seamen on deck was the usual run of things. The firemen in the *John Hardie* were Chinese which is the reason why they had their own cook.

It would appear that the Hardie brothers did not hold steamships in very great esteem. Although they did purchase a second one three years later, their real interest remained in sail tonnage.

*　　*　　*　　*　　*　　*　　*

Returning to the *Archibald Russell*, one month was occupied in discharging her cargo and preparing for her next voyage. On July 11th, with Captain Lowe still in command, she was taken in tow for Hamburg to load for Sydney. The passage took five days and after docking she was very soon in trouble. During a summer gale, she broke adrift from her moorings and drove down on the steam coaster *Die Reine*, causing damage to her rails and also to the rudder of a barge in the vicinity. The *Archibald Russell* sustained some damage to her own rails and was taken to a shipyard for repairs. Six days later, she was towed to her loading berth.

Hamburg at this time was a great port for sailing ships. Germany still had faith in the future of sail and was buying up discarded British ships and building large barques for the nitrate trade from Chile. One Hamburg firm was operating two huge five-masted vessels which regularly made fast passages to and from the west coast of South America with steamships' regularity. The *Archibald Russell*, with her painted ports, seemed archaic as she lay among the larger German ships of more progressive design.

She sailed from Hamburg on August 31st. The foremast hands were almost entirely foreigners. Mrs. Lowe signed on again for another voyage and a stewardess was engaged to make life less lonely for her. This woman was forty-one years old and the wife of the cook.

On September 9th, the *Archibald Russell* passed Prawle Point and 25 days out, on October 4th, was reported in a position 7°N by the schooner *St Clemens*. She arrived in Sydney after 109 days on December 16th, 1906. There were twelve desertions including the Second Mate, and the First Mate left at his own request. After discharging, she was chartered to load wheat. The *Vimeira* was also in Sydney loading for home. She had come out from Hamburg in 102 days and sailed on January 10th for Falmouth. The *Archibald Russell* followed her six weeks later on February 21st.

On March 21st in the Roaring Forties a Russian seaman, Ivan Petroff, fifty-five, fell overboard and was drowned. The incident is best described in the Captain's own words as he wrote it in the official log.

> Lat. 54°14′S. Long. 129°10′W. This is to certify that Ivan Petroff, A.B., was washed or fell overboard this morning at 8.35 from the sheerpole of mizzen topmast backstays. He and apprentice Dickens were there coiling up the running gear that was washing about in the water on the maindeck. It was blowing a strong gale from the west, with a high cross sea running at the time. It had blown with hurricane force from the north during the night. While Petroff and Dickens were coiling up the gear (lee) in the rigging, she shipped a heavy sea to windward and gave a violent lurch or roll to leeward at the same time, putting the sheerpoles aft in the water. No-one saw Petroff go, although Dickens was beside him he did not see him fall or washed away until the ship was steady again and partially free of water, then he missed him, he reported to myself and the 2nd Mate said that he was *afraid* Petroff was washed or fallen overboard. As it was blowing a strong gale and fearful sea running at the time it was impossible to try and rescue him and the ship would be a mile from him ere he was missed. The ship was

Plate 24 The Archibald Russell. *Roaring Forties.*
C. Beneke

doing about 10½ knots at the time and sea and wind too heavy to think about putting a boat out. Got his effects aft and will sell them by auction the first fine day.

So wrote the Captain, and the entry was duly signed by the Mate. Such entries were usually read out to the crew for approval since to leave a shipmate to his death in the ocean was a sad and serious affair, even though weather conditions made a rescue attempt out of the question. One can imagine the old Captain sitting at the saloon table pondering over the wording of the entry while the ship, straining and lurching in the heavy seas, raced on before the storm. Later, with the crew assembled on the quarterdeck, their oilskins wet and glistening with spray, he read out the words from the log. When the day came for the auction, the deceased seaman's effects realised a paltry £1.7s.4d. In cases where a seaman died, his personal property was always auctioned to the crew and the money handed to the authorities at the port of discharge.

71 days out, she was spoken in the Atlantic 1° north of the Equator and on June 6th, dropped anchor in Falmouth Roads, after a passage of 105 days. Two days later she was on her way to Antwerp where she arrived on the 12th.

The *Vimeira*, which had preceded her to Falmouth by 7 weeks, beat the *Archibald Russell* by 7 days with her passage of 98. It is worth saying something about the *Vimeira* here. She was an attractive ship with painted ports and deep single topgallants. She served Hardies faithfully for 33 years and seems to have kept out of any serious trouble, and although she never made a reputation for herself as a fast ship, she was a steady passage-maker. A study of her voyaging shows that she did on occasion produce a good passage.

On her maiden voyage in 1891 with Captain Steven in command, she sailed out to Calcutta from Birkenhead in 94 days and home again in 109. Her best Australian passage was 93 days from Melbourne to Plymouth in the year 1900, which is as good as one would expect from a ship of her class. In 1896, she made a very lengthy passage of 190 days with case-oil from Philadelphia to the Japanese port of Hiogo. While employed in this, in the early morning of November 4th, as she was approaching the coast of Sumatra, 115 days out from Philadelphia, a small boat was sighted making signs of distress, which turned out to be a ship's gig with half a dozen people on board including one woman.[1] When they came aboard, Captain Steven learned that they were survivors from the full-rigged ship *Avoca* and that the lady was the wife of the Master who was also in the boat.

*Plate 25 The V*imeira
A.D. Edwardes Collection, State Library of South Australia

They had been cast adrift for several days after having to abandon the
Avoca in a hurry when she caught fire three weeks out from Calcutta.
Later in the day, they sighted another boat with a further nine of the
Avoca's crew on board. The *Avoca* belonged to James Nourse & Co., who
engaged in transporting coolie labour from Calcutta to the West Indies, but
fortunately at the time she was without coolies, carrying only a jute cargo,
otherwise Captain Steven might have been in trouble with two or three
hundred coolies on board and all the extra mouths to feed, as it took the
Vimeira 37 days to sail the 900 miles to Batavia which entailed navigating
the narrow Straits of Sunda. Having landed the survivors, the *Vimeira*
wandered on for a further 45 days, threading her way through the
archipelagoes of the East Indies to Hiogo, which lies at the eastern end of
the Inland Sea some 2,500 miles distant from Batavia.

Leaving the *Vimeira* and returning to the *Archibald Russell*, which it will
be remembered had just arrived in Falmouth, the tow up the Scheldt to
Antwerp was not uneventful. The German steamship *Helgoland* was coming down river bound for Bremen when she struck the *Archibald Russell*
on her port side. She also raked the barque's rigging, damaging masts and
yards. A survey in Antwerp showed that several plates were set in. How-

ever, after discharging her cargo this damage was put right and in September, she lay in Antwerp's Siberia Dock in company with the full-rigged ship *Arctic Stream*. Both vessels were idle pending the end of a dock strike, the *Archibald Russell* waiting to be towed round to Hamburg to load for Santa Rosalia in the Gulf of California.

The *Arctic Stream* was in the news at this time. She also had just completed a voyage from Sydney. Captain H.M. Dixon, a well-known Master in his day, had undertaken to race the crack German training ship *Herzogin Sophie Charlotte* back to Europe. There was much speculation about the contest in Sydney and substantial bets were placed. Both ships left port with a flourish, spurning the use of tugs. All along, the German was the clear favourite, but in spite of this the *Arctic Stream* won by three days, confounding most people as she sailed with a scratch crew of 28 men against the training ship's complement of 80.[2]

The *Archibald Russell* finally sailed from Antwerp for Hamburg on September 7th. Captain Lowe left, his place being taken by Captain Swinton.

Chapter VIII

Captains Swinton and McMillan

Captain Swinton was a Scot like all the *Archibald Russell*'s Masters under the Red Ensign. From his photograph he looks to have been a man of strong character. He was in his fifty-second year and had been in command of sailing ships since he was twenty-six. He came from Pathead in Midlothian. His first command in 1881 was the brig *Globe* which he unfortunately lost the same year when she foundered in the South Atlantic on a voyage from Newcastle to Valparaiso with a cargo of coal. Subsequently, he joined Thomas Law & Co.'s Shire Line and commanded five of their ships successfully. He was seven years in the barque *Banffshire* until 1887, followed by two years in the full-rigged ship *Morayshire*, which disappeared with all hands shortly after he left her, while on a voyage from Java to Vancouver. From 1892 to 1899, he commanded the four-masted barque *Buteshire*. He came to the *Archibald Russell* from the fine skysail yard four-masted barque *Dumfriesshire*.[1]

The *Archibald Russell* sailed from Hamburg with a coal cargo on October 2nd, 1907, for Santa Rosalia. The passage occupied 145 days, which might seem lengthy, but Santa Rosalia is 350 miles up the Gulf of California, a narrow stretch of water with the wind blowing directly out of it. She took nine days from Hamburg to Falmouth and was next sighted approaching the Straits of Le Maire, not far from Cape Horn, by the brand new s/s *Maori* of the Union Steam Ship Company of New Zealand, homeward bound on her maiden voyage. She took a further 54 days to the entrance of the Gulf of California and spent the next 19 days beating wearily up to her destination, anchoring on February 24th, 1908.

She was four months in Santa Rosalia discharging her coal, during which time the cook, carpenter and eight seamen deserted, leaving their wages behind them such as they were. This sort of thing happened quite often. It was accepted and even welcomed by some, especially if the men were troublesome. It also had the advantage of saving on the men's wages while the ship was still in port. One of the apprentices also deserted and another, Norman Goodwin, an Australian from Sydney, packed and left for home on hearing of the death of his father. When the cargo was discharged, ballast was loaded and the fore and mizzen royal yards were sent down. Some replacements for the deserters were procured, but she now had only 22 of the original crew to work her up the coast. She sailed on

Plate 26 Captain Swinton
Mrs M.S. Marshall

71

June 21st for Port Townsend at the entrance to Puget Sound in search of a homeward cargo.

In Port Townsend, there were further changes in the crew. The senior apprentice, Thomas Salmond, had completed his indenture and, with Captain Swinton's permission, took himself off to Canada where he made his way to the nearest Mercantile Marine Office and sat for his Second Mate's Certificate. Four months later, he sought out his old ship which was then in Tacoma and was duly signed on as Second Mate, the previous man having left at his own request in Port Townsend. This was a smile of fortune on young Salmond; or was it? With the New World before him, he could have chosen easier ships with better pay and conditions: lumber schooners, Pacific Island traders or coasting steamers. But perhaps he liked the *Archibald Russell*. Anyway, he remained in her another four years, completing three voyages, the last one as First Mate.

Time dragged on however, with cargoes hard to find, and altogether the *Archibald Russell* was eight months on the coast. During this barren period in her life, she was not alone. Many other sailing ships on the Californian coast were in the same predicament or even worse. Homeward cargoes were offering but at ridiculously low rates, too low to show any profit. Nitrates from Chile at 12/6 per ton had fallen to half what it was twelve months previously, while the rate for grain from Puget Sound homewards

Plate 27 The Archibald Russell *at Tacoma*
A.D. Edwardes Collection, State Library of South Australia

to the United Kingdom had plummeted from 33/9 in 1907 to 15/- in 1909.[2] The masts of the laid-up ships graced the creeks and backwaters of the Sound, their crews paid off or deserted.

The shipping industry was in the throes of one of the worst depressions in history. Due to the high level of activity in the shipyards of Europe, the supply of ships overran the demand as owners took delivery of large numbers of tramp steamers. World tramp tonnage increased by 46% between 1900 and 1914, and freights fell everywhere to the lowest ever. In some respects, the *Archibald Russell* was fortunate. There were ships which had been laid-up for a year or even two. At this time, a comparatively new sailing ship could be bought for a song, the prospect was so bleak.

Eventually however, the *Archibald Russell* did obtain a charter. This was a grain cargo, possibly barley. The highest rate offered homewards this year from Puget Sound was 27/6, but it varied with the season and the reluctance of the sailing ship owners to take up low paid charters may have forced the rate upwards a little as the granaries filled with the summer crop. But, whatever the rate was, she finally loaded and sailed on December 29th, 1908.

The homeward passage started badly. Five weeks after sailing, they had only progressed 1,800 miles and were in the region of the lonely Revilla Gigedo Islands when a passenger, who had been in the ship since she sailed from Hamburg, committed suicide. His name was Erskine, 41 years old, from Montrose. Presumably he had joined the ship for the good of his health, not uncommon in those days, but how or why he took his life remains a mystery. The passage stretched out to 175 days, the ship not being spoken until the Western Approaches, 161 days out. Fifteen days later, she was off Falmouth, where she received her orders and, without anchoring, set course for Dublin, arriving on June 22nd, 1909.

This voyage had taken the best part of two years during which the *Archibald Russell* had carried only two cargoes, and with freight rates being so low it is doubtful if she made much, if any, profit for her owners.

Captain Swinton left in Dublin. He was not in good health and never went to sea again. A relief Master came to take her under tow to Port Talbot, where she was chartered to load coal for another voyage to the west coast of South America.

In spite of the recent seemingly poor voyage, the Hardie brothers considered that trading conditions were going to improve. In this they were correct and started to expand their fleet again, even though other sailing ship owners were discarding theirs, either going out of business altogether or turning to steam. In this year of 1909, they purchased the barques *Kil-*

meny, Killoran and *Kildalton* from the firm of James Browne. These were handy little barques built by the Ailsa Shipbuilding Co., of Troon, the best known being the *Killoran* which had a long and useful life about which we shall hear more. The *Kilmeny* was the odd one out. She came off the stocks in 1894 and was 100 tons smaller than the other two. The *Killoran* was built in 1900 and the *Kildalton* in 1903, the latter being different inasmuch as she was given ballast tanks, something common enough in steamships but rare in a sailer. In the *Kildalton*'s case, the ballast tanks were confined to fore-peak and after-peak, of 43 tons and 36 tons respectively, not enough to allow her to sail empty without solid ballast, but perhaps sufficient to hold her upright in port with holds swept clean. Any saving on solid ballast was important, since it all had to be bought in some form or another and this ate up the profits. It could consist of sand or shingle which might be sold at the end of the passage or perhaps rubble of some sort which had to be got rid of somehow by paying for its removal or by dumping at sea. The *Archibald Russell* needed 1,500 tons of ballast for a deep-sea passage and even when loaded with timber, required 550 tons to make her sufficiently stable.

Hardies also took over the management of six ships belonging to the firm of D. Corsar and Sons, a Liverpool firm which was winding up its business. One was a four-masted barque called the *Pegasus*, 2,564 net tons. Two of them, the *Monkbarns* and the *Fairport* of 1,771 and 1,857 net tons respectively, were full-rigged ships; another two, the *Almora*, 1,769 and the *Musselcrag*, 1,871 were barques; the sixth and last of these was the *Chiltonford*, a four-masted barque of 2,198 net tons. None of the Corsar's ships remained under Hardies' management very long.

This was the year John Hardie & Co. purchased their second steamship which was named the *Caldergrove*. She was built at the same yard of William Hamilton & Co., and had the same dimensions as the *John Hardie*. In the same year the old iron full-rigged ship *Brambletye* was sold to the breakers, leaving Hardies with a fleet of fifteen ships under their management.

* * * * * * *

The *Archibald Russell* was six weeks loading a coal cargo for the West Coast. The man who was to command her for the next four years joined on August 20th, 1909. Captain McMillan, a fifty-eight-year-old Scot from Irvine, had just completed two years as Master of the *Hougomont*. Like most of Hardies' Captains, he was an experienced seaman who could be

74

relied on to make steady passages and keep the ship out of trouble. Records show that from 1881 to 1889 he commanded the full-rigged ship *Canterbury* belonging to Patrick Henderson's Albion Line in the New Zealand trade. Henderson threw in his lot with Shaw Savill in 1882 and McMillan sailed in the *Canterbury* under the houseflag of the Shaw Savill & Albion Line until 1889, transferring to the four-masted barque *Hinemoa* the following year. The *Hinemoa*, according to Basil Lubbock, was specially built for the frozen meat trade. He only remained in her five months, forsaking sail for steam in 1892. After ten years, during which he commanded steamships in the Atlantic trade, he returned once more to sail in 1903, in command of Shaw Savill's four-masted barque *Belfast*. 1907 found him in command of the *Hougomont*.[3]

The *Archibald Russell* sailed on September 5th for Tocopilla. A tug was employed to tow her clear of the narrow waters of the Bristol Channel. When the tow rope was cast off near Lundy, and while the hands were making sail, a stowaway appeared, having hidden himself under one of the bunks in the fo'c'sle until the coast was clear. When everything was coiled down and the course set, he was brought before the Captain. He gave his name as Charles Watson of Holyhead, fifty-seven years old, asserting that he was a seaman and willing to do any work required of him. He was a welcome addition to the ship as several men had failed to join before sailing and the crew numbered only thirty including six apprentices. There was also one passenger voyaging for the good of his health.

After clearing home waters she was reported by a passing ship in Latitude 13°N, 27°W, 18 days out and again 4 days later. She was reported once more 46 days out in 29°S, 46°W, bowling along in the trades, but was not sighted again during the passage round Cape Horn, nor in the Pacific until she reached her destination.

On his previous voyage to Tocopilla in the four-masted barque *Hougomont*, Captain McMillan had an unpleasant experience. It was a nightmare come true, a misfortune which could haunt any Master making these Pacific coast ports. He had sailed from Newcastle, N.S.W. with a cargo for Coquimbo, further down the coast from Tocopilla. With the cargo safely discharged, Captain McMillan set sail for the short run up the coast to Tocopilla to load nitrate for Europe. The ship was almost within sight of her destination when the wind fell away and Captain McMillan and the ship's company had the mortification of drifting helplessly past their destination in the grip of the north-going Humboldt Current with no opportunity of regaining their lost ground. The ship was in light ballast

Plate 28 The Hougomont
A.D. Edwardes Collection, State Library of South Australia

condition, compatible with the needs of a short run up the coast and a fair wind, and all effort to make headway to windward was unavailing. Captain McMillan decided it was pointless to waste further time, so he abandoned his charter, turned the bows of the ship westwards and set sail for Australia.[4] However, he did not have the same problem this time and the *Archibald Russell* arrived at Tocopilla on December 1st, 1909, after a smart passage of 87 days.

This voyage was surprisingly trouble-free. In some respects, she had quite an exceptional crew. All but five of the thirty members were British, which did not necessarily mean it was a good one, but at any rate there were only two desertions during this voyage apart from an apprentice who disappeared in Port Talbot. Furthermore, the logbook showed that no disciplinary measures had to be taken against any of the crew during the whole period of the articles. This may have been due in part to the First Mate, a type of officer rare in sailing ships at this time when most young men were turning to a more prosperous future in steamships. Mr. Thompson was a man of thirty, whose previous position had been First Mate of the White Star training vessel *Mersey*, a full-rigged ship manned by sixty cadets. He held an Extra Master's square-rigged certificate and was lieutenant in the Royal Navy Reserve. Under his orderly management, the ship ran smoothly and efficiently.

It took two months for the *Archibald Russell* to discharge her cargo and load nitrates. When it was time to sail, Captain McMillan cast around for new men to bring his crew up to strength. Apparently there were no seamen available in Tocopilla. At any rate, none came forward and he was forced to approach someone who undertook to provide four seamen for £3 per head blood money. These men were undoubtedly shanghaied. Surprisingly, Captain McMillan entered this dubious transaction in the logbook and the British Consul in Tocopilla put his official stamp on the entry. On February 9th, she sailed for Europe and was 115 days to Hamburg, arriving on June 4th, 1910 The crew, having received their wages, signed off and went their diverse ways. Of the stowaway who had appeared off Lundy however, there is no mention apart from the initial entry in the logbook. Some time during the voyage, he disappeared as quietly as he had come, not meriting any further entry in the record, nor reward for his labours.

Captain McMillan's next voyage was to Australia and back. The *Archibald Russell* sailed from Hamburg on August 24th, but made a bad start, taking twelve days to beat down channel and was reported off Plymouth on September 5th. She was spoken 8°N of the Line, 38 days out by the s/s *Lime Branch* and 10 days later was sighted in 10°S by the brig *Francesco C*, arriving at Melbourne on December 4th, 102 days out of Hamburg. She remained 10 weeks in Melbourne, sailing with wheat for Queenstown on February 12th, 1911. She made a good time round Cape Horn and was reported 3°N of the Line by the s/s *Merchant,* 67 days out and would have made an excellent passage had she maintained her speed, but such is the luck of the game, unfavourable winds delayed her and she did not make Queenstown until 99 days out, on May 22nd. She lay there 9 days, during which time the Captain's wife Jeanne and daughter Mary joined for the run up channel to Dunkirk, where she arrived on June 12th.

The following voyage, she was chartered to load timber at the Swedish port of Sundsvall in the Gulf of Bothnia. Sixteen men were signed on for the run to the Baltic. She sailed from Dunkirk under tow of the tug *Arcona* on July 11th, reaching Sundsvall on July 21st. She was there 6 weeks loading a full cargo of timber including deck cargo, and with her crew completed by the addition of a number of Swedish seamen, she sailed for Australia on August 31st, 1911. She was reported 16 days later off Start Point and 41 days out she was again reported by the barque *Pangani* off the Martin Vaz Islands, making good headway in the south-east trades. She reached Cape Otway on December 16th, 91 days from Start Point, and docked the following day at Geelong. After discharging her timber, she was towed to Melbourne to load grain for the United Kingdom. Eleven men deserted during this period, and who could blame them with the higher wages prevailing down under? Wages for Australian seamen were now double those on British ships and men had to be signed on at £6 per month, leaving the Captain and Mate the only ones better paid, a source of some irritation to those who remained with the ship. She sailed on February 24th, 1912, dropping anchor in Carrick Roads, Falmouth, 112 days out on June 15th. Orders were received for Cardiff and the screw tug *White Rose* took her in tow on the 19th, docking in Cardiff the following day. The *Vimeira* was already in Cardiff loading for Rio and was towed to sea on July 3rd. For the next two years, these two ships kept company, their charters bringing them to the same ports, and they were so evenly matched in speed that their sailings and arrivals often coincided.

Captain McMillan's fourth voyage was his last in the *Archibald Russell*. After discharging her grain cargo, she was moved under the tips and commenced loading coal for Rio de Janeiro. A new First Mate joined this voyage, a man well known in the Australian trade. John Cameron came from the clipper *Loch Broom*, having spent a lifetime in sail. Altogether he stayed seven years in the *Archibald Russell,* seeing her through the perilous war years. He was something of a character whom Frank Bowen, the nautical historian, considered worthy of mentioning in his *Ships of the London River*. According to him, Cameron was a really fine seaman, admired by the apprentices for his careful attention to their training. He never suffered unseamanlike behaviour, but may not always have been an easy man to get on with as far as the crew were concerned, judging by the number of desertions. The voyage after he left, desertions dropped off considerably. He was still remembered in Melbourne 30 years later.

The *Archibald Russell* sailed from Cardiff on July 30th, 1912, arriving at Rio 45 days out on September 13th. The *Vimeira* was already there after a 46-day passage from Swansea. The *Killoran* had also paid a visit but sailed two weeks previously bound round Cape Horn to Astoria. All three brought in coal and sailed in ballast. The *Archibald Russell* got away one week before the *Vimeira* on November 13th, but they both arrived in South Australia on January 19th, 1913, 67 and 56 days out respectively.

These colonial voyages were always popular with the British sailor. There was no language problem; if the weather was not always good, at least it was better than the English climate; the beer was good, entertainments just like home; and if the Australian men were not always friendly to the 'pommy', the girls seemed to like them.

More to the point for some sailors, it was the right place to desert from an unhappy ship after a hard voyage, with the opportunities Australia had to offer in the way of better ships, good jobs on shore and better money all to be had for the taking. Quite a number of the *Archibald Russell*'s crew took the chance at different times.

The *Archibald Russell*'s loading port was Port Pirie which was enjoying a boom period. Large quantities of ore, mined locally, were being exported, much of it finding its way to Germany. The port also enjoyed a boom of desertions, mostly from sailing ships, as many as 200 in one year,[5] and the *Archibald Russell*'s crew helped to swell the numbers on her visit. The township itself was unusual to English eyes, something like a frontier town, one wide main street with a railroad running through. The ships' masts towered above the buildings.

It is not certain what the *Archibald Russell* loaded on this voyage, but since she had to be fumigated before taking on any cargo, it points to grain rather than ore. Unfortunately, during the fumigation fire broke out, spreading to the accommodation under the poop, but it was soon under control. The damage cannot have been serious as she loaded and sailed soon after on February 20th, 1913. She made a poor passage homeward of 135 days to Queenstown. The *Vimeira* was only marginally better to Barry with 134 days from Adelaide. The *Archibald Russell* proceeded to Dunkirk where Captain McMillan left and went into retirement. He was sixty-two years old.

If the Australian trade was popular with the sailor, so it must have been with the shipowner. The freight homeward in 1913 was as high as 43/9, and with the outward freight of 19/6 per ton to Rio with coal, a good profit was to be expected. In spite of this upturn in trade, most shipowners continued to dispose of their sailing ships to foreign flags and invest in steam, but those still operating them were entering a period where very high returns on their investments could be expected. There were a few British firms who clung tenaciously to their sailing ships: Thomas Law of Glasgow, Donald Rose of Aberdeen, T.A. Shute of Liverpool and others. Wherever cargoes were available, their ships gathered: the *Elginshire*, the *Mount Stewart*, the *Monkbarns*, the *Kilmallie*, the *Juteopolis* and the training ship *Medway*, to name a few which sailed on in the twilight years.

During the four previous years, five of the ships managed by J. Hardie & Co. passed to other owners. Except in the case of the four-masted barque *Chiltonford*, Hardies only managed Corsar's ships for one voyage each before they were disposed of elsewhere. The *Pegasus* was the first to be disposed of in 1910, followed by the *Musselcrag* and the *Fairport* the same year and the *Almora* in 1911. These four ships passed to Norwegian owners who, at this time by virtue of lower wages, were able to operate sailing ships with greater profit. The *Monkbarns*, however, passed to the London firm of John Stewart & Co. in 1911 for the sum of £4,850. They retained their interest in sail tonnage and kept the *Monkbarns* sailing until 1926.

The *Chiltonford* completed three voyages under Hardies' houseflag. The first, from April 1908 to March 1910, included a passage of 190 days from Hamburg to Santa Rosalia, a coal cargo from Newcastle, N.S.W. to Valparaiso, followed by nitrates to Rotterdam, the whole voyage occupying 22 months and 19 days. Her Master on this voyage was Captain Thomas Atkins who later commanded the *Eudora* and Sir William Garthwaite's four-masted barque *Juteopolis*. He was followed by Captain Robert Montgomery.

Plate 29 The Chiltonford
National Maritime Museum

Chapter IX

Captain Robert Montgomery

Captain Robert Montgomery was a native of Ardrossan and thirty-four years old at the time. His early years had been spent in sail, changing over to steam from 1904 to 1907. However, he returned to sail in command of the *Arranmore*.[1] He was reputed to be a good commander, keeping his ship well turned out. He also took great interest in his apprentices, training them in their duties, especially boatwork in which he set great store. Whenever the opportunity arose, he arranged pulling races between ships.[2]

By his account, the *Chiltonford* was no flyer. She sailed from Rotterdam on May 4th, 1910, with a cargo of coke and pig iron for San Francisco. A month later she was reported 8°N of the Equator in Longitude 29°W. From there she made a course which took her east of the Falklands, arriving off Cape Horn in midwinter. She met gales from south-west to north-west which kept her beating back and forth for three weeks, reaching Latitude 65°S before getting a favourable slant. During this period of continual storm she lost two boats, sustained damage to her steering gear, lost all her headsails, foresail and six other sails. She finally reached San Francisco after 176 days according to Captain Montgomery's reckoning (Hardies' voyage records give 171 days), having not seen land the whole time. The food was all but finished and the chronometer reading was found to be four minutes in error, a matter of 60 minutes of Longitude. The cargo was discharged at Oakland Wharf, after which the *Chiltonford* was towed up to Port Costa to load barley. There followed an uneventful passage of 149 days to Leith, the round voyage lasting a whole year almost to the day.

The last voyage of the *Chiltonford* under Hardies' houseflag commenced with a tow from Leith to Hudiksvall where she was chartered to load a timber cargo to Sydney. Before leaving Leith, she was loaded with 500 tons of pig iron, the minimum stiffening required for the tow to Hudiksvall and also to give stability to the timber cargo. The tow took 7 days. It was midsummer when the *Chiltonford* made port and Captain Montgomery noted that as they towed up to the sawmill, the townsfolk were out in their boats with musical instruments, playing and singing while enjoying the long, warm, summer evening.

The *Chiltonford* was the best part of six weeks at Hudiksvall before she set sail for Australia. From August 2nd to 20th, she encountered calms and head winds before clearing the Danish coast. She was reported off Cape Wrath on the 28th, battling against south-westerly gales. Captain Montgomery recorded a fine run down to 8°N, where the *Chiltonford* was becalmed for a week with eight other ships including the *Monkbarns*. She eventually arrived at Newcastle, N.S.W., 148 days out from Hudiksvall. The homeward voyage from Sydney, N.S.W., with grain to Falmouth for orders occupied 142 days. On August 12th, 1912, the day after arriving at the discharging port of Dunkirk, the *Chiltonford* was sold to G. Windrum & Co., of Liverpool. James Hardie promised Captain Montgomery command of the *Archibald Russell* on her return from Australia. Meanwhile, he did a voyage on the s/s *Ben Vrackie* to fill in time.

The barques *Kilmeny*, *Killoran* and *Kildalton*, purchased from J. Browne & Co., remained in the fleet, tramping around the oceans after whatever cargoes were available, mainly in the South America, Australia, United Kingdom triangle. The *Killoran* and the *Kildalton* carried a fair cargo—3,000 tons apiece—but although their barque rig was not skimped inasmuch as they set royals above topgallants, they were very modest passage-makers.

The *Kildalton*'s 203 days from Glasgow to Port Townsend was something of a monumentally long one under Captain T. Jones, who had her for the first voyage under Hardies' houseflag. She had a change of Masters each voyage which didn't improve her passage-making. In 1913, under Captain T. Dagwell, she sailed outward to Rio with a cargo of cement in 59 days. The cargo was discharged by the crew, bag by bag, using hand-operated 'dolly' winches. She was then prepared for a passage to the West Coast. Although the *Kildalton* was fitted with ballast tanks, Captain Dagwell didn't believe in such new-fangled things. He had the royal yards sent down and took aboard a quantity of earth ballast which appeared insufficient when she reached the strong winds off Cape Horn; according to a member of the crew she 'just lay down to the squalls' as he put it.* The result was a slow passage which took 71 days to Taltal. She loaded saltpetre at Junin and came home to Plymouth in 149 days.

Returning to Captain Montgomery, when he completed his voyage in the s/s *Ben Vrackie*, he crossed over to Dunkirk to take command of the *Archibald Russell*. On July 28th, she was taken in tow for Barry where a coal charter for Buenos Aires was waiting for her. There was quite a gathering of Hardies' ships in port with her at the time; the *Hougomont* was there, the *Killoran* also, both chartered with coal for the River Plate. The *Archibald Russell* signed articles on August 18th for a voyage to the 'Brazils', which in fact meant Buenos Aires and thence to any place offer-

---

*Captain R.W.C. Lamont's account of the *Kildalton*'s voyage appeared in *Sea Breezes*, July, 1947.

Plate 30   Captain Robert Montgomery (1879-1951)
San Francisco Maritime Natural History Park
Robert Montgomery Collection

Plate 31   The Killoran
John Clarkson

ing a profitable cargo. The ship was well-manned with a crew of 38, including 8 apprentices and the Captain's wife of twenty-eight years and daughter of eight months. The last two were signed on as stewardess and assistant stewardess at one shilling per month each. John Cameron signed on again as Mate. The Second Mate was George Fullilove, a Londoner, twenty-one years old, who had just left the barque *Pinmore*. He stayed with Hardies and eventually rose to become Master. The sailmaker, Duncan McRae, had been in the ship since her maiden voyage and was now a permanent fixture. The carpenter, J. Page from Guernsey, previously sailed in the four-masted barque *Thistlebank*. The rest of the crew were Scottish, English and Irish with a sprinkling of Scandinavians. The cook was sixty-two, a Swede from Stockholm. He also came from the *Thistlebank*.

The wages in sailing ships at this time were as follows:

1st Mate	£10	per month
2nd Mate	£7	
Carpenter	£6.10/-	
Sailmaker	£5	
Bosun	£5	
A.B.	£4.10/-	
O.S.	£3	

By themselves, such figures tell us relatively little, but in comparison a skilled craftsman ashore such as a shipwright, a boiler-maker or a blacksmith would be paid a flat rate of between £9 and £10 per month. This must be seen in context with prices prevailing at that time: Woodbine cigarettes 5d for 25; beer 2d a pint; a bottle of whisky 3/6; a 3lb loaf of bread 3d; and a filling meal for a working man could cost as little as 5d.

The *Archibald Russell* left Barry under tow of the tug *T.A. Jolliffe* on September 6th, and there followed a leisurely voyage to Buenos Aires. Shortly after leaving port, the carpenter was laid up with a complaint which the Captain diagnosed as 'erisipulus' (sic), the swellings being treated with iodine and poultices of moist flour, followed by a dose of castor oil. The carpenter soon got tired of this treatment and resumed duties at his own request, saying he would sooner work than be confined to his room any more.

The *Archibald Russell* arrived at Buenos Aires on November 5th, 1913. The other three ships, sailing from Cardiff at varying times, arrived at Montevideo within a month of one another, their times being close and just as leisurely as the *Archibald Russell*'s 60 days:

Hougomont	59 days
Killoran	64 days
Vimeira	65 days

The *Archibald Russell* had not been long in port when an outbreak of dysentery on board laid low several members of the crew. It was a sad time for the Captain and his wife because their daughter, now aged eleven months, also contracted dysentery and died on November 21st. The event cast a gloom over the ship. Four members of the crew were absent without leave and were entered in the logbook as deserters. Meanwhile, the discharge of the coal went on and after the New Year, on January 2nd, she sailed in ballast for Australia. She had a frustrating start; from pilot to pilot she was 54 days in passage, making Semaphore Point off Adelaide on February 25th, 1914. The *Vimeira* came in on the same day, 55 days from Montevideo. They both received orders to proceed to Newcastle, N.S.W. to load coal for Antofagasta. The *Vimeira* was 19 days getting round to Newcastle, the *Archibald Russell* 20. The *Killoran* was already there loading coal for Caldera.

The *Archibald Russell*'s carpenter had a brush with the Captain when he refused to clean out the donkey boiler. It was a Sunday as it happened and he saw no reason why he should work on the Sabbath. A few days later he was in trouble again when, although supposed to be sick at the time and off-duty, he went ashore in working hours. He was fined 5/- for this offence. Altogether, ten seamen deserted in Newcastle. They were replaced by Australians.

On May 13th, 1914, the *Archibald Russell* and the *Vimeira* set sail from Newcastle for Antofagasta. Some rivalry must have existed between the two ships, as the two Captains and members of their crews were sure to have met during their stay in Newcastle. On this occasion the honours were equal. Captain Montgomery steered southwards, making his easting in the Roaring Forties and arriving at Antofagasta on June 29th, after a smart passage of 47 days.* Captain Thomson in the *Vimeira* presumably took the same route, making an equally good passage reaching Antofagasta on the same day. After discharging their coal, they sailed up the coast to load nitrates, the *Archibald Russell* at Tocopilla, the *Vimeira* at Caleta Buena. The *Vimeira* got away first, but the *Archibald Russell*'s loading was delayed and she was still in port when war was declared. Four men deserted and a German seaman was paid off. Captain Montgomery had great difficulty purchasing enough provisions for the homeward passage. Steamers which used to call regularly at ports on the West Coast with supplies were diverted elsewhere or became casualties of enemy action and many commodities were in short supply as a result. He bought what he could, hoping for a quick passage home or help from some passing ship. It was a gamble which did not pay off. On December 2nd, 1914, the *Archibald Russell* sailed for Britain.

She made a slow passage round the Horn and on February 2nd, in Latitude 30°04′S, Longitude 17°04′W, the Captain noted in his log that supplies of tea had run out. Butter and marmalade were also finished and the crew had to be issued with honey as a substitute. The members of the halfdeck were reputed to be the hungriest members of the crew and it is not surprising that Allen Noble, an eighteen-year-old apprentice, was feeling the strain. Mr. Cameron found it necessary to bring him before the Master, charging him with insolent behaviour. Captain Montgomery tried to reason with him, but he was so distraught that he told both men that he didn't give a bugger for either of them. When warned that he might not get a good reference if he failed to moderate his behaviour, he replied with some heat that they could stuff their references up their arses, strong language indeed, all recorded in the official log. He was fined 5/- for this. Later, in a more contrite mood, he admitted that he had been unreasonable. Perhaps

---

*A discrepancy appears here between Lloyds' and Hardies' records, probably due to crossing the date-line.

Mrs. Montgomery was able to calm his troubled brow. The rest of the crew took the additional hardship of short rations with remarkable stoicism.

A sharp lookout was constantly kept for any steamship or sailer from which they might obtain much needed stores, but there was an unusual dearth of shipping. One reason for this was the sinkings by the German armed merchant cruisers *Kronprinz Wilhelm* and *Prinz Eitel Fredrich*. In actual fact, the *Archibald Russell* and her crew were in considerable danger from the latter. The first casualty which overtook Hardies' fleet was the sinking of their barque *Kildalton* by the *Prinz Eitel Fredrich* on December 12th, 1914, off the island of Juan Fernandez.[3]

The *Kildalton*, it will be remembered, had made a lengthy passage from Junin to Plymouth. She went round to Liverpool to discharge. Her Master, Captain Dagwell, left and Hardies had difficulty in finding a suitable replacement for him, but eventually got in touch with Captain William Sharp who had been her Master when she sailed under J. Browne & Co's houseflag. He was sixty-six years old and had already retired, but agreed to do another voyage. The *Kildalton* sailed from Liverpool on September 8th and by November she was battling her way around Cape Horn in very heavy weather. On December 12th, a steamship hove in sight, which turned out to be the *Prinz Eitel Fredrich* on a raiding mission. She ordered the *Kildalton* to heave to, and with the mainyard backed she waited while the German boarding party rummaged around to see if there was anything of value to them, but there was nothing; the crew was taken aboard the raider and the *Kildalton* was sent to the bottom. Her crew spent 19 days aboard the raider and were then put ashore on Easter Island where the *Prinz Eitel Fredrich* anchored in order to take on coal from a captured French barque. She then sailed, leaving the *Kildalton*'s crew to their own devices until they were rescued two months later. Captain Sharp made his way back to Britain and was soon outward bound again in the full-rigged ship *Wray Castle* belonging to the Liverpool firm of R. Thomas & Co.

The *Prinz Eitel Fredrich* doubled the Horn and on February 12th, she sank the barque *Invercoe*, the s/s *Mary Ada Short* and Ropner's tramp steamer the *Willerby*, and according to the *Archibald Russell*'s log, the cruiser must have crossed her path at some time without a sighting.

Returning to the *Archibald Russell*, on March 1st, when just north of the Equator, the s/s *Upo-mendi*, a turret deck vessel registered at Bilbao, hove to in answer to her distress signals. She gave them all the food she could spare, but being short herself she could only give 28 lbs of butter, 4½ lbs of tea, 80 kilos of flour, some tins of sardines and a carcass of mutton, all of which was whacked out amongst the crew.

By now the crew were getting weak with hunger. A deputation of seamen came aft complaining that they could no longer do a full day's work and required a reduction in their hours. It was impossible to reduce those necessary for the navigation of the ship, but normally they were expected to do maintenance work on the decks and rigging during daylight hours. Captain Montgomery allowed them to start one hour later in the morning and work was clewed up in the afternoon half an hour earlier. On March 10th their luck was in when the s/s *Lapland* of Liverpool hove in sight and gave them two weeks' supplies. The Captain, with some satisfaction, noted in the log the commodities received: tins of milk, corned beef, sacks of potatoes, flour, sugar and butter.

On April 4th, having sailed clear of lurking U-boats in the Western Approaches, they made Queenstown, the passage from Tocopilla having taken 123 days. However, their troubles were not completely over and now began a long wait while the naval control decided when it was safe for vessels to leave for their port of discharge. The *Monkbarns* was there, also the barque *Invergarry* (later to become the *Garthgarry*) and the four-masted barque *Galgate* from San Francisco, loaded with barley. In mid-May, the weather was unsettled with gales and during a heavy squall the *Galgate* parted her cables and blew down to leewards on the *Archibald Russell*, whose anchors fortunately held.

The pandemonium can be imagined as the two lofty vessels came together with their sides grinding against each other and the blocks and yards clattering and banging overhead, while the crew were unable to do much to prevent the damage which was bound to result. Eventually, the *Galgate* went clear and, still out of control, drifted ashore while the *Archibald Russell*'s cables held fast.

Altogether, she swung at anchor for two months and finally, on June 12th, sailed for Glasgow to discharge, as it was deemed too risky to send a defenceless ship up channel to Rotterdam with submarines sinking ships right and left. She arrived in the Clyde three days later.

In the meantime, the *Vimeira*, having sailed homeward from Caleta Buena in 108 days, had delivered her nitrates to Rotterdam and then sailed over to New York in 30 days. She was already loading for Australia while the *Archibald Russell* was having her problems in Queenstown. They never again had an opportunity to try their paces against each other.

Captain Montgomery left in Glasgow on June 17th and went into steamships. Seven years later, he returned briefly to the *Archibald Russell*.

Chapter X

The War Years

The new Master was Captain Alexander Buchan, an Aberdonian who had commanded sailing ships for the previous twenty years. The *County of Roxburgh*, the *County of Caithness* and the *Inveresk* were three of his charges and his records show voyages to China, Japan, the Pacific Coast, the United States and the Colonies. In one of his early voyages, he had the misfortune to break a leg which set badly, leaving him somewhat crippled. As a result of this deformity, he became a withdrawn and lonely man. His personality comes through to us more clearly than that of the *Archibald Russell*'s other Masters, thanks to one of her apprentices, Ralph Rogerson, who sailed with him on a voyage to Mejillones in 1919.

Captain Buchan joined the ship in his fifty-fifth year. He appears through the mists of time as a stockily built man with a definite limp, rather aloof in manner but at heart kind and considerate. His reasonable attitude was, on occasion, construed as softness by some of his crews and at times they tried to take advantage of him, but for the most part his voyages were free from serious trouble and although he never beat any records, at least his passages were average. He kept very much to himself during the long voyages. The Master's quarters under the poop were comfortable and self-contained and no-one except the steward entered the saloon without invitation. This aloofness was fairly general on sailing ships; it did not always make for a happy one, but it did give a sense of supreme authority to the Master, who often had to make decisions of life or death.

On August 5th, 1915, Captain Buchan took the *Archibald Russell* from the Clyde on a tramping voyage which kept her away from the United Kingdom for several years. In fact, the nearest she came to her home port was Bordeaux, spending much of the war in waters where U-boats were less active. There was a great deal of money being made by sailing ships at this time. Freights were sky high and anything that could carry cargo made great profits, but the toll through enemy action was disastrous, especially to sailing vessels. August was a particularly bad month with 49 merchant ships lost. Although most of the submarine activity was centred around an area between the Fastnet and Ushant, the *Archibald Russell* was able to sail clear into the Atlantic and lose herself in its vastness. Other sailing ships in the preceding months had been less fortunate than her. The full-rigged ships *Glenholm* and *Crown of India* and the Scottish four-mast-

Plate 32 The Clevedon
National Maritime Museum

ed barque *Dumfriesshire,* Captain Swinton's old ship, were sunk, also the barque *Sunlight,*[1] a vessel which came off the stocks two years after the *Archibald Russell,* which had been used for carrying palm oil in bulk for the Lever Soap Factory and was given the same name as the famous bars of hard soap used in so many households in Britain.

At this time, when the world was involved in a struggle which pledged one side to sink any shipping in sight, whether warship or peaceful merchantman, a man in a remote Baltic port was building up a fleet of sailing ships, slowly and painfully, with great dedication, and there was to come a time when the *Archibald Russell* would interest him greatly. His name was Gustaf Erikson.

Hardies had secured a replacement for the *Kildalton* earlier in the year. On April 28th, they took over the management, on behalf of the British Shipping Controller, of the German ship *Elfrieda,* a prize of war which happened to be in Bristol at the outbreak. They gave her the name *Clevedon* after the watering place nearby and sent her across the Atlantic to Gulfport in the Gulf of Mexico for a cargo of timber.

The *Archibald Russell* sailed with a crew of thirty-three, including six apprentices. Mr. Cameron signed on again as Mate and the sailmaker,

Duncan McRae, was also there. There was no Second Mate signed on at the start of the voyage.

Captain Buchan took a northerly route towards New York. On August 14th, she was in Latitude 49°50′N, Longitude 30°12′W, almost halfway across the Atlantic, 9 days out. By August 28th, she was in Latitude 40°03′N, Longitude 63°57′W and 4 days later, after a passage of 27 days from Greenock, she arrived at New York where she docked in Erie Basin.

New York was booming. With factories at home deeply involved in the war effort, America was now exporting to Britain's old customers everywhere possible and vessels were crowding into United States ports cashing in on an abundance of good cargoes offering at high freight rates. The *Kilmeny* joined the *Archibald Russell*, arriving from Belfast on October 25th, after a passage of 37 days to load for Fremantle. Earlier in the year the *Hougomont* and the *Vimeira* came to New York to load cargoes for Australia. Further south, the *Clevedon* was plodding back and forth across the Atlantic between Mexican Gulf ports and the United Kingdom, laden with Oregon logs.

After the *Archibald Russell* discharged her ballast, she commenced loading for Australia. It was not long after her safe arrival had been reported to Hardies at 11, Bothwell Street, that another report came in telling them that their steamer *John Hardie*, on passage from Java to Glasgow with a cargo of sugar, had been sunk 98 miles west of Cape Finisterre. She was stopped by a German U-boat which ordered the crew to take to the lifeboats, after which shells were pumped into her hull until she sank. Fortunately, there was no loss of life.*

There were no further sinkings among Hardies' ships in 1915, but there were some mishaps. The *Hougomont*, while making New York, encountered dense fog and ran aground on Fire Island where she remained for 13 days before being towed off. The *Killoran* was in collision with a steamship in January at Falmouth while awaiting orders for her port of discharge, and then, outward bound for Valparaiso on the following voyage, she arrived in a damaged condition apparently having encountered bad weather off the Horn. Her Captain, David Reid, died soon after. On her return to the United Kingdom, she joined the *Clevedon* in the log trade from the Gulf of Mexico. For this she had ports cut in each bow through which the logs were passed, making the loading easier.

The *Clevedon* had trouble with her foremast which came adrift when

---

*Captain Bryce, one-time Master of the four-masted barque *Pyrenees*, was in command at this time.

Plate 33 The Hougomont
Strathclyde Regional Archives

outward bound from Birkenhead to the Gulf in December. The heel of the lower-mast crumpled, causing the mast to sink in its step, after which the shrouds and stays became slack, and in this state she was forced to turn back to Falmouth for repairs. Rust seems to have been the cause of all this, which is not surprising since she was forty-three years old. She was soon repaired and six weeks later was on her way again across the Atlantic to Port Arthur on the Sabine River, where she arrived after a passage of 53 days from Falmouth.

Trouble with the *Clevedon*'s rigging seems to have dogged her right from the start of her life when she was the *Chrysomene* belonging to W.H. Fernie & Sons. Built of iron in 1873 and launched from the yard of W.H. Potter of Liverpool, the firm which built the famous *Wanderer*, she was rigged in the fashion of the day with single topgallant yards, and lanyards and deadeyes on the shrouds and backstays. Her first dismasting occurred a year later in 1874, when engaged in the Australian emigrant trade. Towards the end of the war, she was again in trouble with her rigging, but more of that later.

On board the *Archibald Russell*, the men who had given no apparent trouble on the outward trip now started to play up. Crew trouble frequently dogged Captain Buchan when he made port, the log book being filled with entries of seamen drunk and disorderly, absent without leave or in trouble with the police.

One particular offender was the cook, a coloured man called Henry Cowell. He fancied himself considerably and was heard laying down the law about what he would or would not do. He boasted that when the ship reached Australia, he was going to have a high old time, since the Captain would be unable to sack him because of the White Australia policy. On September 7th, Captain Buchan recorded that there was no breakfast for the crew as the cook was drunk. Quite naturally the men were put out about this, seeing no reason to work without their food. The following day, the crew began to disappear, some of them never to return. One morning a few days later, Captain Buchan was stumping up and down on the poop taking his morning exercise when he noticed the cook and the steward engaged in a heated argument. Unable to best the steward in verbal exchange, the cook retired to the galley and a moment later emerged with a butcher's cleaver in his hand, making his way purposefully aft with the intention of threatening the steward with his life. Fearing that a lot of blood was going to be spilled, Captain Buchan quickly called Mr. Cameron. That trusty old seaman responded faithfully and between the two of them they managed to disarm the cook after a struggle. Such behaviour was too much even for the placid Captain Buchan, who had tolerated the cook's nonsense for too long already, and the man was paid off.

Whatever antics the crew got up to in port, they settled down well at sea and there were no further entries in the log book other than those concerning sickness. By New Year's Day, 1916, they had passed the longitude of the Cape of Good Hope, running their easting down just south of the 40th parallel. A coloured seaman, signed on in New York, Victor Soumi by name, was causing Captain Buchan some concern. In the warmer latitudes, this young man showed no sign of illness, but in the cold, damp Roaring Forties, he came aft complaining of symptoms which the Captain diagnosed as tuberculosis. He put him on light duties for the rest of the run to Melbourne.

Towards the end of January, 1916, they were in the stormy waters of the Bass Strait and on February 1st, anchored in the quarantine station off Melbourne, 93 days out of New York. Later she was towed into Victoria Dock. The doctor confirmed the Captain's diagnosis on Soumi, who was immediately sent ashore to hospital. Although he was signed off, the ship hadn't seen the last of him and it was decided to repatriate him by sending him home in a category known as Distressed British Seaman, more commonly referred to as D.B.S. It was also decided to send him home in the *Archibald Russell*.

After discharging her cargo she loaded wheat, sailing on March 30th for Queenstown. 40 days later, she was off the Falkland Islands. The Captain was still fussing over Soumi. On the face of it, it did not seem a wise decision to send him home in a ship bound round Cape Horn, but tuberculosis sufferers were known to benefit from the life under sail and this certainly seemed to be the case with Soumi. The whole episode shows that Captain Buchan had a good heart under his rugged exterior, for he looked after his patient well. He housed him in one of the cabins under the poop, gave him the most nourishing food possible in a sailing ship and a glass of port daily. As the ship reached warmer latitudes, Soumi's health began to improve. This attention to Soumi generated feelings of jealousy in some of the men in the fo'c'sle and one or two of the seamen feigned sickness in the hope of similar treatment. The thought that one of their kind was lording it in the comfort of the after cabin with better food was a bitter pill to swallow while they were sloshing around the decks in Cape Horn weather. But it didn't work. After a cursory inspection, the Captain accused them of malingering and ordered them back to duty.

By the end of June, 1916, the *Archibald Russell* was nearing the Western Approaches where the shipping lanes converged and German submarines waited. Of the ever dwindling band of British sailing ships, the four-masted barque *Bengairn* was sunk in March, followed by the loss of the full-rigger *Cardonia* and the barques *Ravenhill* and *Inverlyon*. May saw the end of the *Galgate*, repaired after her collision with the *Archibald Russell* and now outward bound again. Numerous other neutral sailing ships, many of them recently purchased from British owners, were also being sunk now that Germany had turned to unrestricted warfare and was sinking ships of all nationalities. With these dangers in mind, Captain Buchan decided to try to avoid such a fate if he could and accordingly, on nearing the Western Approaches, he steered for the Azores in the hope of obtaining orders to go to a port away from the danger area. On July 2nd, the anchor was dropped off St Michael. The ship was only there a few hours, during which time she received orders to proceed to Bordeaux. She arrived in the Gironde on July 26th, her cargo being consigned to Pauillac.

After 118 days at sea, the crew decided to have a good time. The logbook became filled with incidents. They complained of bad treatment and poor food. Drink was mainly the cause and the Second Mate, a Swedish seaman promoted to the job for want of a qualified man, appeared to be the ringleader, adopting a truculent attitude towards the Captain. At one

94

point some of the crew broke into the galley and smashed up the cooking utensils. Several refused duty completely, loafing around the decks, skylarking about, hoisting the yards, setting sail and generally out of control, while Captain Buchan watched from the poop without being able to prevent them. The assistance of the French police was requested but when the gendarmes came down, they decided that what was going on aboard the *Archibald Russell* was none of their affair. One can imagine their amusement at the sailors' antics and their departure with Gallic shrugs of their shoulders. No meals were cooked on board as the steward and cook were afraid to go to the galley and the officers were forced to go ashore for their food. However, discipline was eventually restored and the deserters brought back by the police. Soumi, now seemingly recovered, left the ship and so did the obnoxious Second Mate, who was replaced by promoting one of the apprentices, James Bruce.

She sailed from Pauillac for New York on September 21st, making what turned out to be a lengthy passage. At the start, the winds were fair and light and she took 14 days to cover the first thousand miles. Then she battled with contrary winds for the rest of the way, arriving at New York on November 15th, 55 days out. The voyage was officially ended, the crew being paid off and new articles opened. Several of the old hands signed on for another voyage. However, it was not easy to find replacements for the others, although wages had gone up more than double in some cases and were now as follows:

1st Mate	£20 per month
2nd Mate	£16.10s
Carpenter	£16
Sailmaker	£15
Able Seaman	£12

Overtime was paid but only in port, the rate being 9d per hour, except on Sunday when it rose to 1/-. The officers were paid at the same rate as the men.

A cargo consisting of lubricating oil, gasoline, refined petroleum and turpentine[2] was loaded in New York this time and the New Year of 1917 found the *Archibald Russell* loaded and ready for sea but short of crew. The snows whipped over the chilly waters of her anchorage off Staten Island while on shore more seamen were assembled. Eventually, they were shipped out to her and on January 9th, she made sail for Fremantle.

On her passage south she ran the gauntlet of the German commerce

95

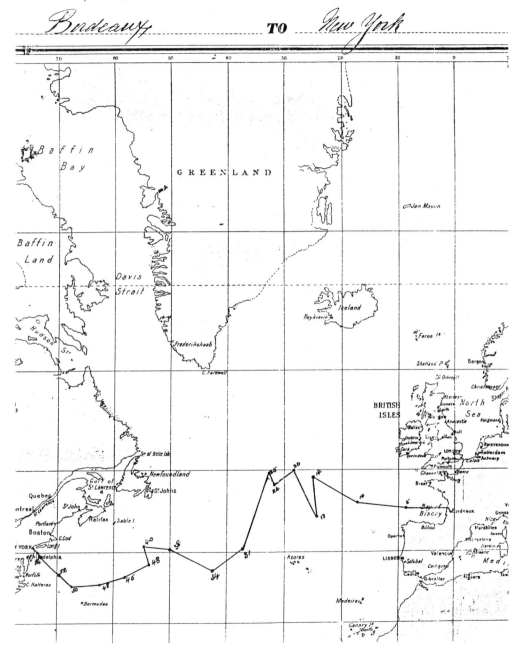

Fig 7   Captain Buchan's track chart, Bordeaux to New York

raiders *Seeadler* and *Möwe* which were operating in the central Atlantic between West Africa and Brazil. The *Seeadler*, an apparently innocent sailing ship, was in reality well-armed and equipped for destroying unsuspecting Allied merchantmen and was commanded by a romantic German naval officer called Count von Luckner, who fancied himself as a twentieth century buccaneer. With two powerful engines and sails she was able to be independent of the shore for long periods and by straddling the sailing ship routes of the oceans, she posed a threat to any slow-moving merchant vessel. The *Möwe* was a full powered steamship and even more successful in disrupting shipping while tying up warships in futile attempts to track her down.

On the day the *Archibald Russell* sailed from New York, the *Seeadler* was off the Azores where she sank two tramp steamers on January 9th, 1917. She then sailed south for St Paul's Rock which lies just north of the Equator, midway between Africa and South America. The French barque *Charles Gounod*, loaded with maize, was her next victim, followed a few days later on January 28th, by the Canadian schooner *Perce* from Halifax to the United Kingdom, loaded with a cargo of lumber and fish. Count von Luckner remained in this vicinity for several weeks hoping for a rich haul in this much frequented part of the sea.

The *Archibald Russell* reached the latitude of St Paul's Rock on February 7th, but her luck held and she slipped by below the horizon without being spotted. The *Seeadler*, casting around for more prizes, was sighted by a neutral vessel, the four-masted barque *Viking*, a Danish training ship equipped with wireless, and Count von Luckner, fearful of being reported to the Royal Navy, sailed south-west towards Rio de Janeiro where he sank the four-masted barque *Pinmore*, a ship in which he had served as a young man, and the barque *British Yeoman* belonging to J. Taylor & Co. of Dundee. Later the *Seeadler* doubled the Horn to be wrecked on the Pacific island of Mopelia.

Meanwhile the *Archibald Russell* was sailing steadily south with the crew ignorant of what was going on around them. On February 15th, she was nearing Trinidad Island and on the same day, not far to the south-west, the *Möwe* was making her way north along a route where the pickings were rich. That day she sank the British steamships *Brecknockshire* and *French Prince* and, had her course taken her a degree or two eastward, she would have sighted the *Archibald Russell* and sunk her.

Soon after this lucky escape, the *Archibald Russell* turned east and by March 3rd, was off Tristan da Cunha. She passed the Cape of Good Hope 66 days out and now, well into the Roaring Forties, her speed picked up, sailing just in excess of 240 miles from noon to noon on March 17th. Two seamen who had signed on in New York tried malingering, saying they were too ill to take the wheel or go aloft. Captain Buchan noted it in the logbook, but if he believed them, their shipmates certainly did not and locked them both out of the fo'c'sle. In these cold and stormy latitudes they found little comfort elsewhere and soon returned to their duties.

On March 30th, she was off St Paul's Island, bearing up for Fremantle. Ahead of her, 400 miles west of Cape Leeuwin, the German commerce raider *Wolf*, a one-time Hansa liner, sank the little Mauritius owned barque *Dee*. The *Wolf* had considerably disrupted shipping by planting mines off Cape Town earlier in the year and sinking ships off the Seychelles and the island of Minikoy. Fortunately she didn't wait around but steamed away across the Great Australian Bight and missed sighting the *Archibald Russell*, which arrived at Fremantle on April 16th, 97 days from New York.

The discharging of her general cargo went on at a leisurely pace. There never seemed to be any sense of urgency in getting the sailing ships to sea, in fact priority was usually given to the steamships in port. Eventually, after two months and one week, she sailed from Fremantle for Cape Town on June 23rd, 1917. Her cargo most likely consisted of railway sleepers made from the wood of the *jarra* tree which is noted for its durability and resistance to ravages by tropical insects. On the day she did sail, she very nearly came to disaster. The wind was fresh when she cleared port. The pilot had been discharged and sail was being made. The Bosun, William Watson, was securing the starboard quarter boat when she shipped a sea which washed him clean overboard. Captain Buchan immediately hove to, sent a man aloft to keep an eye on the Bosun and ordered the port lifeboat away. The boat was launched without trouble and the rescuers soon had him aboard, but when they tried to row back towards the barque they found they could make no headway.

On board the *Archibald Russell*, Captain Buchan watched them anxiously and realised after a while that they could not fetch back. Although on a lee shore they were still several miles off, so he wore ship and bore down, hoping to pick them up, hoist the boat aboard and square away for the open sea. By the time he came up to them, the wind had freshened and the rising sea made it impossible to bring the boat alongside with safety. As the ship surged by, a heaving line was thrown which was quickly made fast, and at the same time Captain Buchan shouted that he would tow them to calmer water.

They had to sail four miles towards the shore before the sea was smooth enough. They were in a perilous position with shallows so close to leewards that they were in danger of going aground, but the boat and crew were quickly hoisted aboard and sail upon sail was piled on as they made for the open sea. By now they were getting close to Rottnest Island and the lookout post there was frantically setting off flares to warn them that they were standing into danger. The wind was too strong for the barque to be put about without bringing the masts down, there was no room to wear and anchoring was out of the question. Captain Buchan did the only thing he could, which was to stand on with as much sail set as possible, steering as close to the wind as she would go, and hope that with luck she would clear the shoal water. The *Archibald Russell* never had the reputation for being a weatherly ship and for a while it was touch and go. Gradually, however, he could see that she was winning clear of danger. It was a near thing and as she swept past, heeling to the gale, her lee scuppers awash, the crew must have drawn many a sigh of relief, as she surely would have left her bones there and some of theirs as well.[3]

After this the wind dropped away and for the next 10 days the ship drifted along covering a bare 200 miles. On July 4th, she found the trade winds which carried her steadily across the Indian Ocean and one month later she was off the south coast of Madagascar. A deputation from the crew came aft complaining of the salt pork which they said was inedible. Captain Buchan agreed that it did seem bad and ordered another barrel to be opened, but this was also found to be off. All the remaining barrels of pork turned out to be bad, having been cured improperly. However, they still had plenty of salt beef and this was issued instead. They were 20 days covering the next 1,200 miles and dropped anchor in Table Bay on August 14th, 52 days out.

She was 5 weeks in Cape Town discharging her cargo and loading ballast for the run to Australia. Across the dock lay an old windjammer putting the finishing touches to her masts and rigging. She was loaded with a coal cargo which had shifted, sending her over on her beam ends. She lost her mainmast, foretopgallant and everything above her mizzentop. She was eventually towed into Cape Town by a Blue Funnel ship. Her name was *Ferreira*,[4] her nationality Portuguese and she was rigged as a barquentine, but none of this could disguise the fact that she was the once famous *Cutty Sark*, fallen on hard times but still earning a living.

The *Archibald Russell*'s crew got up to their old tricks of drinking and being absent without leave, but no-one deserted. Mr. Bruce, the Second Mate, requested to be paid off and one of the able seamen, W. Stewart, was promoted in his place. They sailed for Melbourne on September 21st, arriving 40 days later on October 31st, 1917.

99

The newly-promoted Second Mate jumped ship in Melbourne. Captain Buchan was either unlucky with his junior officers or else expected too much of the men he promoted. Anyway, he appointed another able seaman in his place and the barque set sail for New York. The Admiralty had supplied the Captain with secret orders, presumably concerning courses to steer to avoid German raiders. The day after sailing, he showed these orders to Mr Cameron and noted the fact in the log. The voyage was uneventful apart from an incident involving the Second Mate and an able seaman, H. Ferguson, just before making New York. Ferguson was working on the mizzen lower tops'l yard and was seen to be smoking his pipe. The Second Mate shouted up to him to remove it from his mouth and get on with his work, but all he got was obscene language and a point blank refusal. The seaman further added that he wasn't taking orders from a jumped up A.B. who recently had shared the fo'c'sle with him. The incident was recorded by the Master in the official logbook and Ferguson was duly fined five shillings. The *Archibald Russell* arrived in New York on March 18th, 1918, 90 days from Melbourne. She remained there nearly 3 months, discharging and loading.

New York was still a happy hunting ground for good cargoes and this year a number of British sailing ships came there. The *Hougomont* cleared for Melbourne soon after the *Archibald Russell* docked. The *Kilmeny* sailed for Melbourne on June 2nd, and the *Vimeira* some time later for Sydney. Sir William Garthwaite's four-masted barque *Juteopolis*, the full-rigged ship *Wray Castle* and the barques *Riverford* and *Invergarry* all took cargoes to Australia. Other ships which loaded in New York for Australia were John Stewart & Co's barques *Kilmallie* and *Falkirk*, Thomas Law's barque *Kirkudbrightshire* and the old wool clipper *Mount Stewart*.

Hardies' barque *Killoran*, having completed two voyages from Britain to the Gulf, returning with Oregon logs, sailed for Santos and thence to Wallaroo for a grain cargo. She had her share of good fortune in avoiding the attention of the U-boats, but she had some adventures. On January 22nd, 1917, outward bound, she came across the survivors of the Hain Steamship Company's steamer *Trevean*, 240 miles south-west of the Fastnet. This ship had been captured by a U-boat whose Commander allowed the crew to take to the boats after having made prisoners of the Captain and two gunners; then they placed bombs in her holds which sent her quickly to the bottom. Soon after she sank, along came the *Killoran* and picked up 75 men, some of whom had been torpedoed in another ship and rescued by the *Trevean* not long before she herself was sunk.

Homeward bound the same voyage, the *Killoran* had to call in at Lough

Swilly in the north of Ireland to get her orders and wait for a naval escort. She was off the entrance on the evening of June 15th, and was told to stand off till daylight next day as the port was closed. This was the sort of order given to a steamer, and some officials in their ignorance failed to realise the problems a sailing ship, being subject to the winds, could have when making port. Captain Pyne, the *Killoran's* Master, ignored his orders and ran straight in to anchor off Buncrana, causing something of a flurry amongst the port officials as the boom defence had to be hurriedly opened for him.

On the passage to Santos the following voyage, she was caught in a hurricane and forced to heave to under fore-topmast staysail with a sea-anchor out and oil bags over the bow. As the centre of the storm passed over the ship, the crew experienced difficulty in breathing and the decks were swept clean by the seas time and time again.[5] However, she came through and continued to Santos where she arrived on February 17th, 1918, after a long passage of 107 days.

The last war casualty to the Hardie fleet was the steamer *Caldergrove* which was sunk 200 miles west-north-west of the Fastnet on March 6th, 1917. This was their worst tragedy as she was sent to the bottom without warning by a German submarine with the loss of her Master and 18 of her crew.* She was never replaced and the firm's venture into steamships was over for good.

Returning to the *Archibald Russell* in New York, we find her once again loading for Australia. Her cargo was quite an exceptional one for a sailing ship, inasmuch as it was a general one of many diverse commodities. For some years vessels of the *Archibald Russell's* type had been compelled to accept bulk cargoes with the lower freight rates, while the steamships got the more profitable general cargoes. At this particular time there was a desperate shortage of steam tonnage for charter to Australia, and the obvious alternative choice was to make use of any well-found sailing ship available. The manifests, which are still held in the United States Archives at Washington, D.C., show the cargo to have consisted of just about everything imaginable and it is possible to list only a few items. There were lawn mowers and sewing machines, baby carriages and motor cars, pianos, pianolas and gramophones. There were horseshoes and saddles, agricultural machinery of all sorts, telephones, clocks, clothing, stationery, shotguns, rifles and ammunition, cases of oysters, dental wax, brewer's

---

*Captain McMillan, previously Master of the *Archibald Russell*, was in command. He had been brought back from retirement. He was 70 when he died.

isinglass, clothes wringers, batteries, buttons and blotting paper. All these items and many others were stowed in the hold until it was full and the ship right down to her marks.

The crew had been paid off soon after arrival at New York. As sailing day drew nearer, new articles were opened; several of the previous crew who had worked by in port, signed on again. The ship was now 3 years out of the United Kingdom and the staunch few of the original complement still had a long way to go before they saw their homes again. They sailed for Australia on June 8th, arriving at Sydney on September 22nd, 1918. The passages from New York of the *Vimeira* and the *Hougomont* this year were well matched: the *Vimeira* made 98 days to Melbourne; the *Hougomont* 104. The *Archibald Russell* had further to go to Sydney and made it in 106 days.

At this point Hardies nearly lost the *Hougomont*. She was requisitioned by the Shipping Controller soon after she arrived in Melbourne and ordered to Hong Kong in ballast where she duly arrived on November 13th, 1918. Her fate was to be the same one which several other sailing ships suffered at this stage of the war. There was a need for tankers to carry bulk petroleum in order to meet the increasing demand for fuel for the Royal Navy. The four-masted skysail barque *Owenee* was stripped down almost completely of masts and yards and started work as the motor vessel *Ortina Shell*, and Devitt & Moore's sail training ship *Medway* was treated in the same way, becoming the *Myr Shell* in spite of strong protests by her owners. Others requisitioned, beautiful sailing ships with years of life ahead of them, were the four-masted barques *Howth, Celticburn, Goodrich*, the barque *Dolbadarn Castle* and now the *Hougomont*. The Armistice had been declared when she reached Hong Kong and the need for further tankers was over, but in spite of the protests by Hardies, the wheels of bureaucracy continued to grind on and the process of removing the Hougomont's masts and yards was commenced. Then one day the work ceased. Hardies had managed to gain control of their ship once more. By that time, she had been stripped to her lower masts and the crew had to set to re-rigging her almost completely. However, by early January, 1919, she was once again shipshape and on the 9th she set sail for home. Whether she had cargo on board is not clear; it may have been a general one including tea, but her homeward passage was far from a clipper one. She was off Tandjong Priok at the beginning of February, passing through the Straits of Sunda. On April 26th, she was reported off Ascension Island, finally arriving at London on July 14th, 186 days out from Hong Kong.

In the meantime the *Archibald Russell*, having discharged her cargo, loaded grain for Callao. The logbook shows evidence that the crew had celebrated the Armistice with a drinking spree but there were no desertions this time. She sailed through Sydney Heads for Callao on November 17th, 1918. It was the last time in her career she visited that port. She dropped anchor in Callao Roads after a passage of 54 days on January 10th, 1919.

She was 3 months on the coast discharging her grain and loading a cargo of nitrates. The steward deserted and a Japanese signed on in his place. He came from Hiroshima and turned out to be a great asset to the ship. They sailed from Tocopilla on April 20th, homeward bound at last, and after a passage of 113 days, arrived in the Mersey on August 19th. Two days later she docked at Ellesmere Port, where the crew were paid off. Only 11 of the original 35 members of the crew completed the voyage which had lasted 4 years and 18 days.

Chapter XI

A West Coast Voyage

With the war behind them, J. Hardie & Co. set about getting their ships back into their old trade. Thomas Hardie now directed the affairs of Archibald Russell Ltd, Coalmasters, from 24, Sherbrook Avenue, Pollokshields, while James continued to manage the ships from 11, Bothwell Street. During the war, the ships had earned good profits. The freight rates for the coal cargoes from the United Kingdom to Rio rose from 18/- in 1914 to 90/- per ton towards the end of the war and homeward cargoes of nitrate from Chile from 38/- per ton to 250/-.[1] The general cargoes from New York ended when peace came, but the ships had made a great deal of money for the firm. The *Hougomont* is said to have made £26,500 in one six-month charter.[2] Grain cargoes homewards from Australia could be obtained at 250/- per ton and a cargo of flour from South Australia to New York in 1919 could earn a four-masted barque carrying 4,000 tons, a sum of £32,000. Such high freights were not to last, but in 1919 shortages of

Plate 34   Thomas G. Hardie
Mrs Ethel Hardie

food in Europe kept freights high.

The year 1919 saw all but one of Hardies' ships at a home or Continental port. The *Hougomont* was in London from Hong Kong, the *Vimeira* at Cork 132 days from Sydney, the *Kilmeny* loading coal in Cardiff for Rio and the *Killoran* at Rotterdam. These four ships were sent down to South America to pick up grain cargoes for home. The *Archibald Russell* was discharging her nitrate cargo in Ellesmere Port and the plan for her was a ballast passage outward round the Horn to Chile for another cargo of nitrate. The *Clevedon* at this time was having problems down in the Southern Hemisphere. She had sailed from New York in July for Dublin. Her Master, Captain W. Wakeham, had commanded her since 1915 and under him she plodded across the oceans making steady passages without breaking any records. He had his share of troubles during his years in her and unfortunately was destined never to see the shores of home again.

The dismasting in 1915 has already been mentioned. On her second voyage to Port Arthur for logwood in 1916, she grounded in the Sabine River, but was towed off two days later without serious damage. In 1917, she arrived at Santos after a passage of 79 days from Garston with her coal cargo heated up dangerously. On October 3rd, 1918, she struggled into Durban 92 days from New York, in bad shape after encountering heavy weather on the passage in which she was pooped and her decks swept by a sea which left a trail of damage: her compasses were smashed and washed overboard; the main chainplates fractured leaving shrouds and backstays adrift. Her main tops'l yards came down and the whole mainmast threatened to go overboard. However, she was patched up and set sail for Melbourne arriving February 16th, 1919, 55 days out. In Melbourne she loaded a cargo of wheat and sailed for Callao arriving 54 days later after what must have been a stormy passage, having again sustained some damage, this time to her deck which was stove in, letting sea-water into her cargo. Captain Wakeham, who seems to have been accident-prone, was drowned in the dock at Callao on December 12th, 1918, his place being taken by Captain J. Kavanagh, after which the old *Clevedon*'s luck changed, her remaining two years under the Hardie houseflag being untroubled.

Back in England, the *Archibald Russell*, having discharged her cargo, was preparing for the forthcoming voyage to the West Coast. Captain Buchan was now in his fifty-ninth year and this was to be his last voyage. It was also the last voyage under the Red Ensign in which the *Archibald Russell* was sailed in a manner likely to show a profit.

John Cameron left this voyage. He had been six years in the ship and during this period of faithful service it is doubtful if he had been home

GLASGOW FOLK

MR T. G. HARDIE.

Civilised society is easily made the victim of a word. In this year, 1930, "Rationalisation" is dominant. All our industrial ills are put upon it, all our industrial hopes are centred in it. It is reducing the human labour element in manufacture. That seems at first blush unreasonable. But Rationalisation means industry according to Reason instead of rule of thumb methods, cut-throat competition, and the waste of over-lapping industries.

Like the introduction of machinery, its first effects create individual hardship, but its ultimate outcome promises to extend employment and resuscitate industry.

Mr T. G. Hardie is an authority on the subject. He has been operating it since youth.

His father, well known and honoured in shipping circles, was the late Captain John Hardie, who started ship-owning away back in 1874.

"T. G." as a young man had the job of rationalising the business from the sailing ship to the steamer. That, too, caused dislocation, but it was the energy and determination of the Clyde men that maintained and enhanced the position of the Clyde area.

He remained in the business till 1913, when he transferred his energies to the coal-owning firm of Archibald Russell and Co., Ltd.

In three years he had carried through a great rationalisation scheme by uniting with David Colville's, of Motherwell. He now directs the two concerns, and adds also the Tharsis Sulphur and Copper Co., Ltd., retaining his interest in shipping as a member of the Committee of Management of the British Register of Shipping and Aircraft.

As a young man he was well known in the football field, and for many years played for the Battlefield and Pollokshields Athletic.

Now his inclination is towards yachting, and the West of Scotland, his happiest sailing seas.

Plate 35   Sketch of Thomas G. Hardie

more than once. Hardies gave him command of the *Vimeira* and so, at the age of sixty-two, he at last reached the top of his profession, making some very fair passages in her. His place was taken by a man in his mid-twenties by the name of Masterton.

A young apprentice called Ralph Rogerson, making his first voyage, joined on October 9th, 1919, at Ellesmere Port, where 1,800 tons of ballast were being loaded. Two other apprentices, Hurst and Bruce, had joined the day before. They both came from the training ship H.M.S. *Worcester*, and as Ralph climbed up the gangway he could see them working aloft on the mizzen royal yard. On October 14th, the *Archibald Russell* was towed from Ellesmere Port to Liverpool, where she was dry-docked for cleaning and painting. After this was done she was taken to the Albert Dock to complete the final preparations for the voyage and to sign on the rest of the crew.

By the declining standards of the time, the crew was a good one. There were English, Scottish and Welsh seamen, the only foreigners being a Dutch seaman and the Japanese steward who joined the previous voyage. Several of the seamen were young men who signed on for a voyage in order to qualify for pilotage service, where experience in square-rig was required. The old sailmaker, Duncan McRae, was there, and a man called Willis with a wooden leg signed on as the ship's cook. Finally, to bring the number in the half-deck up to six, three more first-trip apprentices joined: Fisher, Howarth and Coyne. It was rare at this time to have a crew so predominantly British, but only six of the seamen had any real experience in sail.

On November 11th, 1919, the *Archibald Russell* was all ready to sail and was towed out of Albert dock into the Mersey, her destination Taltal. There was a slight delay in this early part of the voyage. It was the first Armistice Day and all traffic was halted to ensure that the two-minute silence was properly observed. When they finally cleared the Mersey the tug had a stiff tow in the face of a fresh breeze from the north-west, with the *Archibald Russell* unable to help by setting sail. As she passed the coast of Anglesey the wind backed to the westward, a quarter which was of no use to a ship in ballast wanting to make her way down St George's Channel, so in the early hours of November 12th, she put into Holyhead. Next day the wind went to the north-north-east and being a fair one Captain Buchan made sail, running her down channel clear into the Atlantic in quick time.

The weather was good for the run down to the Horn, giving the green hands a chance to settle in and learn the ropes. The Equator was crossed 25 days out and on New Year's Day, they passed the Falkland Islands. Captain Buchan shaped a course well to the south, taking her down to Latitude 61°. In spite of it being midsummer in the Southern Hemisphere, it was cold enough for the crew to start complaining and a deputation came aft with a request for coal to light the stove in the fo'c'sle. Captain Buchan demurred at this, pointing out to them that the weather was no different from what they would get in Northern Scotland in summertime, but eventually he relented. One can imagine him shaking his head and saying to himself that sailors were not what they used to be.

By the 63rd day they were round the Horn, having sailed from 50° N to 50°S in 14 days. They encountered some bad weather and were hove

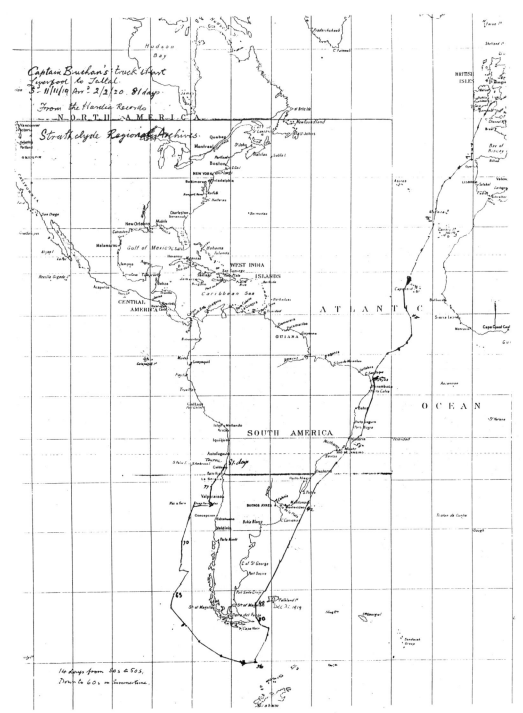

Fig 8   Captain Buchan's track chart, Liverpool to Taltal

to during the worst of it, but once round the corner they made good speed northwards. One of the few indications of the speed of which the *Archibald Russell* was capable comes from Ralph Rogerson whose job it was, with the other apprentices, to heave the log, and his claim of reaching 13½ knots on one occasion is quite a modest one. There was a patent mechanical log on board to record the miles each day for 'dead reckoning', but this was rarely streamed. The time-honoured method was employed with the wooden 'log ship' attached at the end of a line, and a sand glass which was turned as the 'log ship' was hove overboard, the speed being determined by the number of knots which passed through the apprentice's hand when the sand ran out.

According to Hardies' movement book the *Archibald Russell* came to anchor off Taltal on February 2nd, 1920, 81 days out from the Mersey, which must be reckoned to be a good passage. Here she waited until orders were received to sail up the coast to Mejillones. The wind was light on the passage but the current helped them, and on February 9th, they anchored a mile and a half off the port and prepared to discharge their ballast into the sea before loading nitrates.

While the crew dug the ballast out of the hold, the apprentices were employed in other jobs and spared much of the hard work. One of them was kept busy helping the carpenter maintain steam on the donkey-boiler. This was no sinecure as it needed a constant supply of sea-water drawn up in buckets from overside, fresh water being too expensive. Salt water didn't do the old boiler any good and it had to be opened up frequently to scale off the deposit. The other apprentices manned the boat, rowing the Captain ashore daily to do the ship's business which often took some time to complete. They spent the hours in the boat on the Captain's orders as he refused them permission to leave and gave them no money anyway. There was often a swell rolling in at the landing jetty and they had to lie well out clear of the surf. In no way was Captain Buchan going to allow them to 'frequent taverns and alehouses' in violation of the terms of their indentures.

Discharging the ballast and loading nearly 4,000 tons of nitrate occupied two months. The crew were given shore leave only once during this period. The food which was dished up in port was no different from that which they had at sea, and with the monotony in the hold and working at the 'dolly' winches, it is not surprising that the crew started to drift away. There was scant amusement to be had in Mejillones, as the place mainly consisted of white painted adobe huts and little else. When the loading started, the work of stowing nitrate was carried out by one solitary Chilean stevedore working on his own. It is sobering to contemplate the task before this man. 80,000 bags weighing 1 cwt apiece had to be carried by this one toiling individual and placed exactly in position, giving a broad stow at the base, narrowing towards the top to raise the centre of gravity and ease the ship's rolling in a seaway. All this was in the twilight of the hold, each bag placed with confidence that it would not shift, even in most violent weather.

Time hung heavily for the apprentices and they took any opportunity which offered to relieve the monotony. Captain Buchan allowed them to go ship visiting sometimes, although there were fewer ships coming for nitrate these days with the war over. There was a German sailing ship, deep loaded with nitrate, which had lain interned throughout the war and was now waiting to be allotted to one of the allies as reparations. Occasionally they visited ships of the Pacific Steam Navigation Co. which came in, and once they went aboard a Japanese steamer where they were made really welcome, the bonds of friendship between Britain and Japan being very strong at that time after a successful partnership during the war. Altogether these West Coast ports compared unfavourably with the friendly ports of Australia and the romantic harbours of the East, and all on board were heartily glad when the last bag of nitrate was hoisted aboard.

Although the old customs carried out aboard sailing ships were dying, the ceremony of 'Hoisting the Southern Cross' was still observed on the *Archibald Russell*. A large wooden cross was made to which red and white lanterns were fixed at the ends. The cross was hoisted to the masthead when the loading was completed while the crew sang the shanty, 'Hurrah my boys, we're homeward bound'. The ceremony was usually watched by the other sailing ships anchored around who joined in the celebration by ringing their bells and cheering. Sad to say at this time there were no other sailing ships in port to cheer the *Archibald Russell* when her cargo was loaded. Seven years later the last shanty sung to the hoisting of the 'Southern Cross' occurred in the full-rigger *William Mitchell* during the last voyage made by a British sailing ship to the West Coast.[3]

In early April the *Archibald Russell* was loaded. Four Chileans were signed on in place of the deserters. No additional stores were taken aboard, only enough fresh water to see them home, and on April 8th they sailed. During the run down to the Horn the crew were busy preparing the ship for the bad weather which they could expect. Among the numerous tasks the hatches, always vulnerable, had to be securely lashed against being stove in, and life-lines were rigged fore and aft along the decks. During the loading some of the crew, especially the first voyagers, expressed apprehension as the ship sank lower and lower in the water and the freeboard decreased. With 3,800 tons in her she was right down on her marks and before long their fears proved well founded when the seas came tumbling aboard as they reached stormier latitudes. Apart from being frequently drenched when working at the braces, they had the usual difficulty in getting the food from the galley to their quarters and sometimes a meal was lost or spoiled on the way. They rounded Cape Horn in a storm, sighting the peaks between squalls as they rolled their way past.

When they reached the Trades their troubles were soon forgotten. They only spoke to one vessel during the passage. This was a tanker, homeward bound like themselves, with whom they exchanged signals by semaphore. The passage was rather protracted and when nearing the Irish coast, 121 days out, they encountered hazy weather. Captain Buchan was unsure of his position but stood on with a light breeze, making 2 or 3 knots. Suddenly they heard a fog signal and Mizen Head loomed up out of the fog. There followed a few hectic minutes while all hands struggled to get the ship to pay off. They cleared the rocks by a narrow margin and set their course for Queenstown where they anchored next morning, 122 days from Mejillones, on August 8th, 1920.

The crew were now able to enjoy the last few days of the voyage in comparative ease. They lay three days in Queenstown during which time orders came to proceed to the Dutch port of Terneuzen. Sailing in glorious summer weather they made their way slowly but steadily up channel, with every stitch of canvas set. The wind favoured them across the North Sea into the River Scheldt and they did not give their rope to the tug until they were right off the entrance to the Ghent Canal. On the 19th, the *Archibald Russell* was moored in Terneuzen, the voyage ending pleasantly.

Chapter XII

Hard Times

Captain Buchan left in Terneuzen. He had commanded the *Archibald Russell* for five years and was now sixty. He had shown himself to be a steady, reliable Master who managed ship and crew with care and understanding and it is a pity that he didn't remain for the final voyage. Perhaps he realised that everything was changing and that now was the time to go. Had he stayed, it is unlikely that the subsequent voyage would have turned out such a fiasco. His successor was Captain Auld, who had recently completed a voyage in the *Kilmeny* to Canada for a timber cargo, which he brought home from Halifax in the excellent time of 14 days to the Fastnet.

While the *Archibald Russell* was on her voyage to the West Coast, the other ships of the fleet, with the exception of the *Clevedon* which had not yet returned from her long spell of tramping round the world, had made voyages to Buenos Aires outward with coal and home with grain. They made leisurely passages with the exception of the *Vimeira* under Captain John Cameron who now appeared to be the only Master to show any sign of urgency over these post-war voyages.

Hougomont	S'd Northfleet	7.10.19	Arr'd B.A.		6.12.19	60 days
	La Plata	28.1.20	Cork		7.5.20	86 days
Killoran	Cardiff	10.5.19	B.A.		10.7.19	61 days
	B.A.	28.8.19	Rotterdam	29.11.19		93 days
	Antwerp	6.2.20	Monte-			
			video		31.3.20	54 days
	Bahia					
	Blanca	29.5.20	Dublin		24.8.20	87 days
Kilmeny	Cardiff	2.4.19	Rio		23.5.19	51 days
	B.A.	10.9.19	Antwerp		21.12.19	98 days
Vimeira	Queenstown	21.12.19	B.A.		6.2.20	47 days
	La Plata	24.3.20	Queens-			
			town		28.5.20	57 days

The *Clevedon* finally arrived in England with her cargo of nitrate. She came, not by way of Cape Horn but through the Panama Canal, 114 days from Valparaiso.

While freight rates held, these voyages were profitable. In 1919, a

Plate 36 A fate to be avoided.
The four-masted barque Owenee *as the tanker* Ortina Shell.
H.G. Mowat

freight of 60/- could be obtained for coal outward to the River Plate and 270/- per ton for a grain cargo homewards.[1] These rates varied with the season and Hardies may not always have received the top rate, but during this period of post-war recovery, it was possible for the *Hougomont* and the *Vimeira* to earn £64,000 in gross freight during one year's leisurely trading. This situation however did not last long. By 1920, freights had fallen by more than a half and Hardies were looking to Australia again where a grain cargo could be loaded for home at 205/- per ton.

Thus the summer of 1920 saw all the Hardie fleet at United Kingdom ports, apart from the *Archibald Russell* which was discharging her grain at Terneuzen. The *Hougomont*, having unloaded at Cork, went to Swansea to load coal for Santos, while the *Vimeira*, which also discharged at Cork but was unable to get an outward coal cargo, sailed in ballast for Australia, reaching Newcastle, N.S.W. after a passage of 95 days; from there, she loaded for Antofagasta. The *Kilmeny*, after discharging her timber cargo at Garston, sailed for the Gulf of Mexico on October 16th, 1920. No cargo could be procured for the *Killoran* so she was sent out to Australia in ballast with the expectation of some sort of employment and arrived in Adelaide on April 9th, 1921, 115 days out. The *Clevedon* brought her nitrate cargo to Ipswich and, after discharging, towed to Northfleet where she loaded Kentish coal for Buenos Aires.

The *Archibald Russell* once again had to make the outward passage in ballast. This consisted of rubble from demolished buildings, useless save for the humble purpose of enabling an old windjammer to sail 12,000 miles to pick up a cargo of grain for a hungry continent. The voyage was not a success and perhaps never could have been financially, being nothing more than a gesture of the owners who must have known that the end of the sailing ship as a profitable venture was very near. However, the Company was not yet prepared to admit defeat and the ship was duly got ready for another voyage.

The new Master, Captain Auld, was an imposing man of fifty-eight years from Saltcotes, with a stature exceeding 6 ft. Like his predecessor he had suffered an injury to one of his legs and walked with a limp. His appearance on deck in time of stress put fear into troublemakers and he brooked no nonsense from sea lawyers. The First Mate's name was McDonald, a wee chap who kept a revolver ready in case of trouble. John Keir, the Second Mate, had served his apprenticeship with Hardies and had previously sailed in the *Kilmeny* and the *Killoran*. The apprentices returned from their holidays and the seamen, consisting mainly of Dutchmen and Scandinavians, were signed on. The old sailmaker and the carpenter remained another voyage, and so did two Chileans who had joined in Mejillones. The voyage began badly and ill luck dogged the ship all the way to Australia.

The *Archibald Russell* left Terneuzen under tow by the Belgian tug *President de Leeuw* on October 30th, 1920. As they made their way through the Straits of Dover the wind freshened to gale force from the south-west, with the tug struggling to keep the ship from drifting on to the Goodwins. They cleared the Sands but were unable to weather Dungeness, being forced to anchor with the tug steaming ahead to keep the ship from being blown ashore. The gale persisted and the position became more and more desperate, with the shore getting closer. Eventually, another tug was sent out to assist the *President de Leeuw* and with both doing their utmost they towed the ship clear to safety. It was touch and go, and while the anchors were being hove up, one of them was found to have fouled some obstruction. Before the crew were able to part the cable at one of the shackles, the windlass was damaged to an extent beyond their capabilities of repairing.

This was a fine start to the voyage but there was no help for it but to tow her to a convenient port for repairs. Accordingly, on November 2nd, she was brought to anchor in Cowes Roads. She lay there for 18 days while

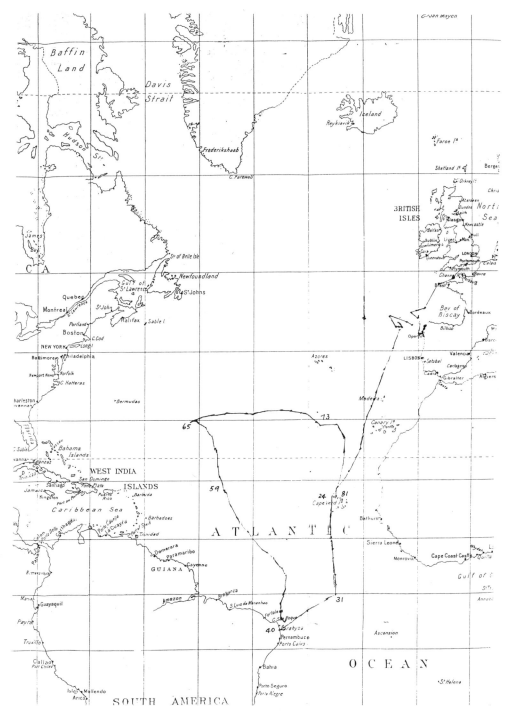

Fig 9   Captain Auld's track chart, Cowes to St Vincent

115

new ground tackle was procured and the windlass seen to.

On November 20th, she once more set out on the long road to Melbourne. For the next 81 days she went unreported and her owners in Glasgow were considerably surprised, and probably dismayed, to get a cable from St. Vincent in the Cape Verde Islands saying that she had arrived there on February 9th, 1921, a mere 2,000 miles away at a time when they could reasonably expect her to be in Australian waters.

What went wrong? Well, nothing serious from the ship's point of view; at least she was sound and the crew in good shape. All had gone well at first after leaving Cowes; they cleared home waters and made their way south, crossing the Equator in 30 days, sighting the shores of Brazil near Cape San Roque. This may have been further west that Captain Auld intended, and now commenced a struggle in light winds against the strong west-going Equatorial current, to get clear of Cape San Roque. In the morning and evening the breezes freshened and the ship was able to make some headway, but when it died the current took charge and bore her westward, losing all she had gained. This struggle went on day after day.

At the same time, not far away, another vessel was engaged in a similar struggle with no better success. This was the full-rigged ship *William Mitchell* of London, on passage from Gulfport to Buenos Aires with a cargo of timber. She reached Cape San Roque on December 26th, and spent the next seven weeks trying in vain to get past the headland. By mid-February she was getting short of provisions and was forced to turn back for Barbados.[2]

It might have been better if Captain Auld had done the same, but he chose to turn north for the Cape Verde Islands. Once again the winds were unkind to him and forced him westward until he was within 600 miles of Bermuda before he was able to turn east, finally coming to anchor off St Vincent, 81 days out from Cowes.

Four days were spent at anchor while messages were exchanged between the ship and the owners. Since no other cargoes were available, it was decided to continue with the voyage to Melbourne. No stores were taken aboard as the ship was adequately stocked, but there was much bargaining for fruit between the crew and the St Vincent boatmen, cigarettes and tobacco being the currency. One or two of the seamen tried to outsmart the boatmen in their trading with empty cigarette tins suitably weighted. When this ruse was discovered, the infuriated boatmen clambered over the bulwarks shouting and gesticulating and a full scale riot was brewing. The Mate, hearing the noise, rushed out on deck waving his revolver to restore order. Somehow the affair was settled and when the ship sailed, apart from the fruit acquired there were four monkeys aboard. The crew eventually were to regret parting with their tobacco as the voyage dragged on and supplies ran out.

On February 14th, they once more put to sea. They experienced poor winds on the run down the Atlantic and progress was unbelievably slow. When they reached the Roaring Forties, two men were frequently required at the wheel to keep the ship before the wind, as she yawed wildly in the heavy seas. The ship was 100 days out from St Vincent when they neared the coast of Australia. Food was getting short, cigarettes and tobacco had long since run out. The lack of smokes caused a great deal of unrest and tempers were short. The Second Mate, while giving orders at the braces, received an insolent reply from a Dutch A.B. and in no time they were fighting hammer and tongs, much to the amusement of the seamen and apprentices who cheered them on, greeting any diversion with enthusiasm. A heaving deck in the Roaring Forties is no place for a scrap and the Second Mate's effort to maintain discipline landed him flat in the scuppers, but determined not to be beaten he was up on his feet, fighting mad. The tall figure of Captain Auld appeared above them on the flying bridge, stopping the fight and sending everyone back to their duties. But bickering continued. The voyage had lasted too long and tempers were understandably frayed.

As they neared the Australian coast, the food shortage became acute with everyone fore and aft on short rations. Then one day the steamship *Walton Hill*, homeward bound, hove in sight and seeing their distress signal, altered course towards them. With the mainyard aback, the crew of the *Archibald Russell* launched the port lifeboat. It was the first time the boat had been waterborne for months as no boat drills had been carried out and the crew had to bale for their lives with the water spurting through the seams; but they managed to keep afloat, returning with carcases of mutton, potatoes and, more important to some of the crew, cigarettes and tobacco. Spirits were high as they rowed back to the barque through the heavy swell. They could see the rest of the crew lining the rails in eager anticipation of having a square meal at last. It was a scene all too common: the rust-streaked, weatherbeaten windjammer, long overdue, lying hove to, rolling easily to the swell, begging provisions from a passing steamer. The *Walton Hill* was generous in what she gave, but the bill for it was certain to be sent to 11, Bothwell Street for payment.

There was about this time some concern at Lloyds over the ship's safety and they were in communication with Hardies, who themselves were not worried. The *Killoran* had just made a lengthy passage of 113 days from

117

the United Kingdom to Australia. They pointed this out to the underwriters and also the fact that the *Archibald Russell* was only 100 days out of St Vincent.

A few days later the *Archibald Russell* was off Cape Borda and Captain Auld managed to signal their arrival, but this was premature as the wind continued to head them and they were blown off the coast again. It was days before they managed to make up the lost ground.

The wind which was foul for the *Archibald Russell* was a fair one for the *Clevedon*. This old ship, now in her forty-eighth year, had sailed from Northfleet three weeks before the *Archibald Russell* left Terneuzen, and in the meantime had run to Buenos Aires in 59 days, discharged her coal cargo there and sailed on to Adelaide in ballast in 62 days. On June 8th, she sailed from Adelaide homeward bound, loaded down with a cargo of grain while the *Archibald Russell* was still struggling to make port without having carried a single cargo to earn her keep. Even now, although only a short distance from her destination, the contrary winds kept her at sea another eight days before she finally reached Melbourne, 205 days out from Terneuzen.

After such a tedious voyage, many of the crew deserted and who could really blame them? They owed no allegiance to a ship which took twice as long as any other to complete a passage, one which only gave them their pound and pint and sometimes not that; a nineteenth century ship trying to make a living in the twentieth. Several were caught but preferred gaol rather than ship out again in a hungry Scottish barque, deep loaded, bound round Cape Horn. She had lost her reputation as a smart ship. The Mates and apprentices remained, also the old sailmaker and the two Chileans, but apart from these, Captain Auld had to scratch around for a new crew.

The ballast was discharged at Williamstown and she was then towed across the Bay to Geelong where she loaded grain for the United Kingdom. While the loading was going on, the *Kilmeny* sailed in from Fremantle.

On July 25th, 1921, with 3,800 tons under her hatches and a fresh crew in the fo'c'sle, the *Archibald Russell* sailed for home. This homeward passage went without any serious problems. She met with some heavy weather off Cape Horn, losing a few sails but otherwise all went well. She made Queenstown on November 17th, 115 days out. It was not a good passage but many ships took a great deal longer this season.

She lay at anchor two weeks off Queenstown. On December 1st, the tug *Vanquisher* commenced to tow her to Cardiff where her grain cargo was consigned. It was a stiff tow against head winds and they did not pass Lundy Island until December 3rd. She finally berthed alongside Spillers

Plate 37 The Archibald Russell. *Storm conditions.*
R. Rasmussen

and Bakers Mill and in the process unfortunately sustained damage to her bowsprit. The crew were paid off and the apprentices sent home on leave.

Some members of the crew may have left her in Cardiff with no regrets, no backward look, glad to see the last of the old windjammer; others, the Master, the Mates, the apprentices with their indentures still uncompleted and the old sailmaker, Duncan McRae, who had stitched every sail in her for 21 years, may have wondered what the future held with ships laying up, owners going out of business and unemployment rising.

The skyline around Cardiff Docks which a few years previously had been dominated by the masts of sailing ships, now had few in evidence. Freights were falling to pre-war levels, but running costs and wages remained high. The post-war boom was over and there was a surplus of tramp steamers whose owners were anxious to carry any cargoes available.

As each ship arrived at her destination, plans were made for eventual laying-up. The *Hougomont* was the first to arrive, docking at St Nazaire on

June 4th. The *Vimeira* under John Cameron made a fast passage of 94 days from Antofagasta, reporting at Queenstown on August 9th, and four days later sailed for Calais to discharge. The *Clevedon* came home in 125 days, anchoring off Falmouth on October 11th, where she received orders for Middlesborough. The *Kilmeny*, although the last to leave, surprisingly made the best passage from Australia of 96 days. The last to arrive was the *Killoran*. She was 36 days to the Horn and 69 days out she crossed the Line, her time being almost as good as that of the *Kilmeny*, but from then on she lost speed and turned up at Ponta Delgada in the Azores 113 days out with her Master, Captain F. Pyne, seriously ill. When the news of this reached Bothwell Street, Hardies sent Captain Watson of the *Hougomont*, which was at that time lying idle at St Nazaire, to take over the command of the *Killoran*. He brought her home from Ponta Delgada in 21 days, arriving at Sunderland on November 29th.

Very little has been written about the *Kilmeny*. Her passages, according to Hardies' movement book, were rarely fast enough to arouse comment yet hardly ever unduly extended and she seems to have led a fairly quiet life during her years under Hardies' houseflag.

The Second Mate on this voyage was one Eben Anderson, erstwhile apprentice in the *Hougomont* under Captain McDonald. Eben's letters give the details of the *Kilmeny*'s last voyage. In 1915, his sense of patriotic duty impelled him to fight for his country. Accordingly, he cancelled his indenture with still eighteen months to go before completion and joined the British Army. He became a machine-gunner and saw action in France where he was wounded. After recovering he soldiered on and was awarded the Military Medal for outstanding bravery. When peace came, he rejoined J. Hardie & Co., doing one voyage in the *Killoran* from Antwerp to Montevideo and home again to Dublin. Soon after this he joined the *Kilmeny*.

The *Kilmeny*'s Master on this voyage, which was to be her last, was Captain George Fullilove, an Orkney Islander, thirty years old, who had previously sailed in the *Archibald Russell* as Second Mate and in the *Hougomont* as First Mate, described by Eben Anderson as a very fine fellow to sail with. The *Kilmeny* left the Mersey under tow on October 16th, 1920. She took 'steam' down the Irish Sea and St George's Channel until the Tuskar was reached, when the tug was cast off and all sail set for a southerly course and a trade wind passage to the Gulf of Mexico. She docked at Sabine Pass on December 3rd, 48 days out from Birkenhead. She loaded a cargo of sulphur, a very heavy one measuring 28 cubic feet per ton which gave her a low centre of gravity since she had no 'tween deck, and Eben recorded that she rolled excessively in any sort of sea, in

Plate 38   The Kilmeny
National Maritime Museum

such a manner as to cause a weakening of the rigging. December 18th found the *Kilmeny* setting sail from the Sabine River for Australia on the start of a tedious passage which lasted 127 days. During this period they endeavoured to cope as best they could with the rolling which threatened to bring down the spars around their ears, and eventually damage to the mainmast forced Captain Fullilove to put into port for repairs. On April 24th, 1921, she docked at Fremantle where repairs were carried out and one month later she sailed for Melbourne where Hardies had managed to procure a general cargo home for her.

Lloyds' Register for 1922 shows that the *Kilmeny* had undergone her second Special Survey No 3 in Antwerp in March, 1920, and now in Melbourne in her twenty-seventh year with her hull, masts and rigging in good order she was reclassified 100 A1, the date being recorded as July, 1921. Without this classificaton she would not have been chartered to carry the general cargo.

By August 18th, 1921, after a six-week stay in Melbourne, the sulphur had been discharged, the homeward cargo loaded and the *Kilmeny* prepared and ready to sail. She slipped through Port Phillip Heads at 4.50 am on the 19th with the ebb tide and a fair wind. Her cargo consisted of casks of tallow, rabbit skins, sheep skins and hundreds of bales of wool. It has been described as a 'clipper' cargo and may have been one of the last wool cargoes taken from South Australia by a sailing ship. It left the *Kilmeny* floating with her plimsoll mark 11 ins above the water and this contributed towards her making one of the best homeward passages of the year out of a fleet which included a number of ships with a reputation for speed. Some credit, however, was due to the enthusiasm of her young Captain and officers who did their utmost to get the best out of her.

The *Kilmeny* had a good start. The winds were strong from the north-east in the Tasman Sea and she was able to make a course well to the south. On the fourth day, she ran 260 miles from noon to noon and on the sixth day, she passed the lonely Auckland Island which lies off the southern tip of New Zealand. In the Roaring Forties, she had good weather and mostly fair winds. There were gales at times, although of no great ferocity, but as Captain Fullilove foretold she met with cold southerly winds blowing straight off the Antarctic Ice Cap, which brought hail and snow. It was still winter in those latitudes south of 50, but that was where the winds were and that is what Captain Fullilove required for a smart passage home.

The Diego Ramirez Islands, just south of Cape Horn, were passed on the 31st day, helped on by a south-westerly gale. The North-East Trades were good and on October 14th, which was the 65th day, she was reported 2°N of the Equator (the name of the reporting ship was not stated in the movement book). But now, after all this good fortune as regards winds, the South-East Trades proved to be poor. The Sargasso Sea gave her frequent calms and progress became slower. In the Westerlies, she experienced a gale which caused Captain Fullilove to heave to under lower topsails.

On the 92nd day out, a report was received from Lloyds at 11, Bothwell Street that the *Kilmeny* had been sighted passing St Catherines. The date was November 17th, 90 days out and the time was 9.30 am. No doubt there was surprise that the *Kilmeny* had beaten the *Archibald Russell* and the *Killoran*, both ships having sailed weeks before her. Six days later she berthed in London. Her passage time has been given variously as 98 days, 96 and 91, this last being Eben Anderson's claim, but according to the dates set down in Hardies' movement book, 96 appears to be the correct one. Nonetheless, the only ship from South Australia to beat this was the four-masted barque *Marlborough Hill* with 91 days from Port Lincoln to Queenstown.

On November 23rd, 1922, at 12.20 pm, the *Kilmeny* entered the Surrey Commercial Dock. Also in dock at the time, discharging a timber cargo from Pensacola, was the old *Cutty Sark*, a ghost of her former glory, with her rig cut down to a barquentine. The *Kilmeny* was moored astern of her, both ships nearly at the end of their sailing days. In 1894, the year in which the *Kilmeny* was launched, the *Cutty Sark* ran home from Sydney to Hull in 93 days. By comparison, the *Kilmeny* was no clipper with her stump topgallant barque rig and full built hull which carried 2,800 tons of cargo against the *Cutty Sark*'s 1,100, but her 96 days passage from Melbourne was no mean achievement, and certainly a feather in the cap of Captain Fullilove and his crew.

This completes the account of the voyaging of J. Hardie & Co's ships when they flew their houseflag. The disposal of the ships by James Hardie was drawn out over three years. It was sad because it was the end of one of the finest and best run sailing fleets of Great Britain. However, three of the ships had most interesting careers under new owners, which we shall follow to their end.

*   *   *   *   *   *   *

Whether a decision had been taken early in 1922 to sell the ships is not known, but preparations were made to lay them all up for the present. The *Archibald Russell* remained in Cardiff over Christmas and the New Year, discharging her cargo. Early in January, her old Captain, Robert Montgomery, who had spent the intervening years in steamships, stepped aboard to take command once again. The place chosen for laying up the *Archibald Russell* was Milford Haven. On January 28th, with Captain Montgomery in charge, she was taken in tow by the tug *White Rose* and the following day arrived at the Haven, where she moored in one of the reaches, together with other ships waiting for an improvement in the market. This was to be her berth for the next two years and was supposed to be a secure one, but as it turned out it had its dangers. The other ships of the fleet were also found laying up berths. The *Hougomont* remained at St Nazaire among a large number of sailing ships, many of them French vessels which had become unprofitable to their owners since the French Bounty Scheme was no longer in operation. The *Vimeira* was given a lay-by berth at Calais, the *Killoran* remained at Sunderland and the *Kilmeny*, after discharging her cargo, was moved to Greenhithe.

The *Clevedon* was the first of the Hardie fleet to be disposed of. It will be remembered that she was not owned by them but only managed on behalf of the British Shipping Controller. On December 16th, 1921, her sale was completed and she was handed over to the firm of Scott, Fell & Co. of Sydney, who were looking for a suitable sailing vessel to convert into a coal hulk for use in the bunkering service of their subsidiary, the Fremantle Coal Company. She set sail from Middlesborough on January 11th, 1922, bound for Fremantle which was to be her base for the next few years. She arrived on March 29th, 74 days out, a good passage for an old timer but one which appears even better on close study, since she was reported off Dungeness on January 23rd, giving her a 67 day passage from departure to arrival. When she reached Fremantle she was stripped down to her lower masts and for the next eight years was towed alongside any coal-burning steamers requiring bunkers. At the end of this period her battered old hull was deemed unfit for any further service even in this humble capacity, and in 1930 she was taken out to sea and scuttled.

It would appear that James Hardie may have contemplated sending his ships to sea again if freight rates rose sufficiently to warrant it, but time went on and this did not occur. The *Kilmeny*, idling her time away at Greenhithe, passed out of Hardies' ownership on May 15th, 1923. She was towed away from her lay-up berth to Germany, where she was broken up.

For a year and a half, the *Archibald Russell* lay in Milford Haven among other ships, and as time passed she became more and more unkempt: seagulls perched in the rigging and fouled her decks; fishing boats passed her by on their way to and from the sea, the fishermen scarcely giving her a glance. She had been there so long, she had become part of the scenery. By now there were sailing ships for sale in every port and many left their berths only for the scrapyard. After eighteen months of this idleness she had not found a buyer, but in June, 1923, an enquiry was made at 11, Bothwell Street from the shipbroking firm of H. Clarkson & Co. of Fenchurch Street, London, on behalf of a Captain Gustaf Erikson for the *Archibald Russell*. The offer was no more than her scrap value, but this did not get a favourable response from James Hardie and although a higher offer was made soon after, nothing came of it. Then in September she was in serious trouble. On the night of the 25th a strong south-westerly gale was causing all the laid-up ships in Milford Haven to ride uneasily at their moorings. The Haven suffers from severe gusts of wind during strong gales; the protecting cliffs seem to hold the wind at bay while the power builds up until it roars over the top down into the desolate reaches beyond, in breathtaking gusts which test a ship's ground tackle to the limit. At the height of the storm, during a particularly severe gust, the 7,000-ton Elder Dempster steamer *Monarch* parted her cables and drifted down on the helpless *Archibald Russell*. She was struck heavily on her port side with a shattering blow which shook the ship from truck to keel, threatening to bring the masts down. Her side was badly dented down to the water-line,

124

frames were set in and rivets started. However, the barque's moorings held and the rigging stood firm. The steamer, completely out of control, blundered on into the night, damaged and leaking and was subsequently beached. By good fortune the *Archibald Russell*'s holds, when sounded, showed no signs of leaks.

November 23rd found the *Archibald Russell* in dry-dock. Captain Erikson, the would-be purchaser, had raised his offer again, providing she was repaired and brought up to her classification of 100 A1. When this was completed, the deal between John Hardie & Co. and Captain Erikson was sealed and on January 3rd, 1924, Lloyds' List announced the sale at a price of £5,000. In actual fact it appears that this was an error and the final price was £7,500, which was a good one for a sailing ship at the time.[3]

Having purchased the *Archibald Russell*, Captain Erikson showed an interest in the three remaining ships and an offer of £9,000 was made by him through Clarksons, but this did not seem to be acceptable to James Hardie. However, he did agree on the sum of £2,650 from Captain Erikson for the *Killoran*, and she was passed on to her new owner on February 23rd, 1924. The *Vimeira* did not find a purchaser willing to put her in commission again. Perhaps her large single topgallant sails and thirty-three years were against her. She was passed to a French firm and broken up soon after.

There now remained only the *Hougomont* rusting away in St Nazaire. Although Captain Erikson's previous offer had been turned down, he eventually clinched a deal with Hardies for £3,000. In her time under Hardies' flag she had had her measure of bad luck which, unfortunately for her new owner, was to continue, finally ending as we shall see in a catastrophic dismasting. With her departure, J. Hardie & Co. ceased to be shipowners, although James continued in business at 11, Bothwell Street as a shipbroker and exporter until his death in 1940, when the firm was closed down.

At the time when Captain Erikson purchased Hardies' last three ships, he already had gathered an impressive fleet of which six were large, deep-water vessels. Three of these had previously flown the Red Ensign: the full-rigged ship *Grace Harwar* of 2,950 tons deadweight, and the four-masted barques *Lawhill*, 4,600 tons and *Olivebank*, 4,400 tons). The others were ex-German sailing ships, the one-time Norddeutscher Lloyd training ship *Herzogin Cecilie* of 4,350 tons and the *Pommern* of 4,050 tons, both four-masters, and finally the barques *Penang* and *Winterhude*, 3,250 tons apiece.

This then was the fleet which the *Archibald Russell* joined in the spring of 1924. In spite of the depression and the competition of tramp steamers, she found a profitable niche with her consorts in the grain trade from Australia to Britain.

During the next ten years, Captain Erikson purchased a further six four-masted barques, including two more discarded training ships, the Belgian *L'Avenir* and the Danish *Viking* of 3,650 and 4,000 tons respectively. There were three from the declining nitrate trade, the *Ponape*, 3,500 tons, the *Pamir*, 4,500 and the *Passat*, 4,700. The *Melbourne*, previously the British *Austrasia*, joined the fleet, as did the American *Moshulu*, a big ship of 4,900 tons, Erikson's final purchase in 1935.

Because of their dwindling numbers and the romance surrounding the sailing ship, these ageing vessels became a particular focus of shiplovers worldwide until eventually their end came through shipwreck, scrapyard or, in a few cases, retirement as museum pieces.

Chapter XIII

Sold Foreign

It was nearly three months after her purchase before the *Archibald Russell* was in a fit state to set sail on the first voyage for her new owner. There is no doubt that he had purchased a fine ship. It has been said that she was one of his favourite vessels. Be this as it may, she was always maintained in first class condition all the years that he owned her, although credit for this must also be given to the Masters and Mates who sailed in her. However, it was necessary to spend a further £1,500 on her before she was ready for sea. She had to be made self-sufficient for long periods of a year or more, since trade could take her to remote parts of the world where only the barest supplies would be available. Much of the gear had to be renewed as there was hardly any left on board. Canvas, rope, wire, barrels of oil and drums of paint were ferried out by barge to her at her moorings in the Haven.[1]

The winter of 1924 was over when the *Archibald Russell*, under the command of Captain Isidor Eriksson, was ready to sail. Worldwide trade was undergoing a terrible slump and no outward cargo was available for her. Ships all over the world were laid up, with freight rates at rock bottom. Thousands of seamen were joining the ranks of the unemployed. Shipowners were reducing wages and cutting their running expenses to the bone. In such an atmosphere of gloom and depression, the *Archibald Russell* was towed to sea on March 8th, 1924. She sailed in ballast from one remote port in the United Kingdom towards another even more remote on the coast of Peru, where she was chartered to load a cargo of guano for the United States. But first she had to call in at Callao for orders. Apart from the blue and white flag of Finland at her gaff, she looked much the same as she did when she sailed under the Red Ensign, for she still carried her painted ports which made her such an attractive-looking ship and she continued in these colours for some time, being one of the few merchant ships sailing the Seven Seas to be painted in this quaint, archaic way.

The passage westward round Cape Horn to Callao occupied 113 days. On arrival on June 30th, she was given orders to sail for the island of Lobos de Tierra, 700 miles further up the coast. Captain Erikson's agents, H. Clarkson & Co., the same firm which negotiated the *Archibald Russell*'s purchase, arranged the guano cargo fixed for discharge at Savannah.

Guano was pretty low on the list of cargoes as far as the ship's personnel was concerned. It consisted of accumulated bird droppings mixed with sand which, over the years, had built up into vast deposits. It was a nauseating commodity: smelled strongly of ammonia; was offensive to nose and eyes; caused corrosion and rotted the ship's sails. Once loading commenced, it was impossible to get away from the smell which pervaded everywhere throughout the ship. Loading points were usually at some isolated, windswept island off the coast of Peru where no real harbour or loading facilities existed. The only labourers were convicts who excavated the guano and shovelled it into bags which were ferried out by barge to the ship, then lifted by means of a whip rove through a block at the yardarm and led down to the donkey engine or manually-operated 'dolly' winch. None the less, the freight of 43/2 per ton was good and certainly satisfactory to Captain Erikson, and the success of the *Archibald Russell*'s venture persuaded him to send others of his ships to the islands, including the *Hougomont* the following year.

Loading occupied about six weeks. When it was time to sail, the Captain set course for the shorter route through the Panama Canal instead of Cape Horn. Time was important even if canal dues were high, as the *Archibald Russell*, if she was going to secure a cargo of the year's wheat crop, had to make her way in the New Year to South Australia where the grain trade which had been depressed for two years was picking up.

On September 12th, she turned up at Panama, was towed clear into the Atlantic side by September 16th, and thence wended her way through the islands. 19 days out of Colon she docked at Savannah in the State of Georgia. The date was October 5th, 1924. Six weeks were occupied discharging the cargo and taking in ballast for the long journey to Australia.

Several of the crew jumped ship on arrival, enticed by good money ashore; their wages on the *Archibald Russell* had been $12 (about £2.10s) per month as able seamen, and those that signed on in place of the deserters had to be paid considerably more. A young American, Carroll Cundiff, twenty-three years old at the time, saw her lying in the Savannah Cotton Dock, spick and span in her new paint and all ready for sea. He decided to sail in her, the spirit of adventure and call of the sea being too strong to resist. He was signed on as ordinary seaman at $30 (£6) per month. Because of his education and air of quiet interest in the ship and her people, he became known as the 'Professor'. The other newcomers were of a different stamp, hard case seamen who signed only for the run to Aus-

Plate 39 Jansen the Swede
Carroll Cundiff

tralia. One of them openly boasted he had killed a policeman while riding the freight cars across the States. However, the Mates on the *Archibald Russell* were seasoned officers and able to handle any material which came their way.

In the early hours of Wednesday, November 15th, 1924, the crew slipped her moorings and cleared Savannah under tow of the tug *F. McCauly*, setting the sails as they went. At 3 am the tow was cast off and the voyage to Australia had begun. There had been no cargo available at Savannah, but in the hold were 1,200 tons of sand ballast, 300 tons less than she usually carried under Hardies' houseflag.

When the regular sea routine of watch and watch was established, the noisome and tedious job of cleaning out the hold was started. The remains of the guano had to be completely removed and the holds made sweet for the wheat cargo. When this was done, the crew were put to chipping the rusty plates and coating them with paint. Carroll found the predominantly Finnish crew easy to get on with and they showed great tolerance in teaching him the ropes. In return, he helped them to improve their English. The cook was an interesting character who was still suffering from the after-

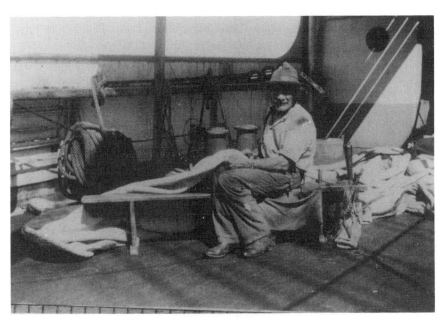

Plate 40 The Sailmaker
Carroll Cundiff

130

Plate 41   Carroll Cundiff and Shipmates
Carroll Cundiff

effects of being torpedoed in the North Sea in mid-winter during the war. In spite of chronic rheumatism and aching teeth, he tried to make the food attractive within his limited means. The Captain had purchased some cheap salt beef from a barque which had been dismasted off the coast of Georgia and come to Savannah in distress. Only by using strong spices could the cook disguise the flavour and make it palatable. He also made a sweet soup from a mixture of dried fruits which was popular with the Finnish seamen. The Captain used to pass the time weaving tapestry and made one of the *Archibald Russell* which eventually ended up in the Mariehamn Museum.

The passage to the Spencer Gulf was uneventful and lengthy, occupying 118 days. Captain Isidor Eriksson made no fast passages during his time in her. First they made their way well into the Atlantic towards the Cape Verde Islands to catch the North-East Trades. The weather was good most of the passage and they ran their easting down north of the 40th parallel, sighting lonely St. Paul's Island in mid-February. They dropped anchor off Port Lincoln on March 18th, 1925. Subsequently, the *Archibald Russell* became well known at this Australian port, loading no fewer than eight cargoes before war brought the trade under sail virtually to a close. The port is situated at the south-western end of the Spencer Gulf, a barren, dusty and sparsely populated place where ships anchored off, waiting their

131

Plate 42   Port Lincoln
A.D. Edwardes Collection, State Library of South Australia

turn to load at the jetty.

She spent two months at Port Lincoln before she was loaded and ready for the sea. It was not simply a matter of taking her berth at the jetty and pouring grain into her holds. First the ballast had to be discharged into the sea by the crew as the cheapest method of getting rid of an unwanted commodity. After this, the shifting boards which divided the ship longitudinally had to be erected to prevent the cargo shifting. Furthermore, some of the ballast had to be retained until sufficient cargo had been loaded to ensure stability. This meant more than one trip to the ballast grounds, since in the shallow waters of the Spencer Gulf the ballast could not be dumped indiscriminately near the jetties. The open anchorage off Port Lincoln was subject to sudden, violent squalls and woe betide any ship caught by one with insufficient stiffening to prevent capsizing. The cargo consisted of grain in bags, some of which were slit to allow the whole cargo to settle in a compact mass. This was known as bleeding. The freight on the cargo was 45/- per ton. While the loading was in process, a four-masted barque came to anchor off Boston Island. It turned out to be the *Herzogin Cecilie* in ballast from Dunkirk.

Just before the *Archibald Russell* completed loading, the *Herzogin Cecilie* moored on the other side of the jetty to load a cargo of grain for Callao. Previously she had been a well-known training ship for the German Norddeutscher Lloyd, but now flew the Erikson houseflag and was sailed very successfully by Captain Reuben de Cloux. She became a household word in Britain, partly because the beauty of this white-painted ship appealed to people during the depressed inter-war years and partly because she made the headlines when she was wrecked off Salcombe in midsummer 1936, in full view of Devon holidaymakers. She towered above the *Archibald Russell*, which in Hardies' old colours and painted ports looked a little drab in comparison. The *Archibald Russell* was short of crew and two of the *Herzogin Cecilie*'s men transferred to her for the run home.

They sailed on May 9th, 1925, at noon, the wind being fair at the time. However, it shifted ahead and they were forced to anchor twice before they cleared the land. In the Tasman Sea they lost the fore and main staysails and main royal in a squall. It was midwinter as they ran through the Roaring Forties, encountering much heavy weather. On July 6th, 58 days out, they passed Cape Horn and on August 6th, when they were in the doldrums, the Italian steamer *Monte Bianco* spoke to them and reported their position to Lloyds. On September 14th, they were approaching Falmouth but the wind became foul and they were forced to run for Queenstown where they

Plate 43 Making fast the main upper topsail
Carroll Cundiff

anchored on September 16th, after a lengthy passage of 130 days.

After six days at anchor, orders were received to proceed to Dublin. In more prosperous days under the Red Ensign there would have been a tug to tow the *Archibald Russell* to the discharging port, but her new owner did not believe in using tugs except where absolutely necessary. Conse-

Plate 44   On the way to Cape Horn
Carroll Cundiff

quently, on September 22nd, she sailed from Queenstown and commenced a weary beat up the Irish Sea against a northerly breeze. It says a great deal for those Finnish deepwatermen: they mostly handled their ships with skill in coastal waters and were rarely in serious trouble. It took them three days to sail the 166 miles to Dublin, tacking ship every watch with the rain tipping down much of the time. They anchored in Dublin Bay at daylight on Friday, September 25th, all hands worn out and disgusted, but glad to be at the end of a tedious voyage.

Tedious it may have been, but for Captain Gustaf Erikson, back in Mariehamn, it was a highly satisfactory one. By now, after eight months of tramping, she had earned over £16,000 in freight, a sum which covered the purchase price and gave her new owner a tidy profit into the bargain. All this at a time when other sailing ship owners were rapidly losing money. The secret of Erikson's success lay in the strict attention to expense. All his ships were well maintained and the crews as well fed as on most ships of other nations. Another factor was that none of his ships was insured, making each voyage a calculated risk. Grain freights varied annually, according to world harvests and the shipping available to transport them. In the case of the *Archibald Russell*, over a ten-year period, she averaged 27/8 per ton homeward from the Spencer Gulf and it could be assumed that this would be a profitable return on Captain Erikson's investment. The occasional outward cargoes helped to boost profits; however, there were some lean years to come during the depths of the shipping depression when freights fell to a disastrously low level.

Plate 45   The Archibald Russell *nearing Queenstown, September 1925*
Carroll Cundiff

Chapter XIV

Mariehamn

After discharging her cargo, the *Archibald Russell* took on ballast and sailed for her new home port of Mariehamn in the Åland Archipelago, to be inspected by her owner who kept a careful check on the maintenance and running of his ships. It also happened to be a suitable place to sign on a new crew and reasonably central for ships to pick up timber cargoes available at Baltic ports. Mariehamn at this time was little more than a village, but her name was to be seen on the counters of numerous sailing ships. Situated on an island among thousands of islets and skerries spread out over the entrance to the Gulf of Bothnia, its sheltered harbour was perfect for laying up ships during periods of idleness. In the winter months, when coastal trade ceased as a result of the icing-up of the ports, it became full of barques, schooners and galeasses waiting for the spring thaw.

The inhabitants of the Åland Islands were largely farmers and seamen, many of whom turned successfully to shipowning. The whole port, which time seemed to have passed by, was absorbed in the business of maintaining a fleet of sailing ships carrying the flag of Finland all over the world. Captain Gustaf Erikson at this time owned the largest fleet of ocean-going sailing ships which practically monopolised the Australian grain trade in sail. His ships also carried a large proportion of Baltic timber, both foreign and coastal. He wielded almost feudal power over the masters, officers and crews in his employ and, although widely respected, he was sometimes referred to in scurrilous terms by those who thought him mean and penny-pinching. It is not borne out by the facts that he was either of these, but he knew his ships and their economies, having served in sail from ship's boy to Master, and had decided views where his money should be spent. He was a Captain turned shipowner and in this respect he was similar to Captain John Hardie. He emerges from the considerable literature about him as a strong character and supreme autocrat, with a firm grasp of the fundamentals of sailing ship management. He was a neatly dressed man of less than average height, with a limp which was the result of a fall from aloft. He was wealthy by Åland standards, although not ostentatious; he owned a car but rode a bicycle; when he travelled abroad, he lived on his own ships when possible.[1] He delegated a great deal of responsibility to his Masters, but he was not above writing them letters in which he reminded them of the best way to mix paints, or advised them on the purchase of stores and

Plate 46 Captain Gustaf Erikson
National Maritime Museum

provisions, or the need for strict economy at all times. His ships were his pride and joy which he was to keep in commission as long as he lived, as he considered that one day the world's oil would run out,[2] and that sail would again return to the oceans in large numbers. There was never a shortage of young men eager to go to sea in his ships and the atmosphere of the harbour and the Sound beyond engendered the desire. During the late summer months, the masts and yards of his deepwatermen dominated the scenery and beckoned the adventurous.

It was to these islands that the *Archibald Russell* came in the autumn of 1925. The approach to the harbour was narrow and rock-bestrewn, requiring both pilot and favourable wind. She took up her berth with anchors down and stern lines made fast to pine trees on the shore. It was late in the season, too late in fact as it turned out, for as she lay in these peaceful surroundings the cold winds from the Arctic were already ruffling the surface of the harbour. Most of the fleet were, by this time, outward bound.

From Mariehamn she sailed up the coast to Sundsvall, where she was chartered to load timber for Melbourne at 85/- per standard. However, events did not turn out as planned. Either the loading of the timber was protracted or the hard winter weather set in before she was ready to sail. She lay there throughout the winter, with the crew dispersed and the snow lying thick on her decks, and was not freed from her bonds until May. This unfortunate and unprofitable period of idleness meant that she would again be late for the season's grain from Australia. It was May 25th, 1926, before she finally got away from Sundsvall and the grain ships were already on their way home with their cargoes, at least those that were able to get them, since the 1926 harvest was a poor one in Australia and there were too many ships chasing too few cargoes.

She arrived in Melbourne on September 30th after a passage of 126 days from Sundsvall. She discharged her cargo there and then shifted over to Geelong to load grain for the United Kingdom at 35/- per ton. During this sojourn in Australia the colour of her hull was changed to white and when painted in this fashion she looked very attractive. She put to sea on January 8th, 1927, and soon after fell in with her old consort the four-masted barque *Hougomont*, under the command of Captain Hägarstrand, now back in the grain trade after her guano droghing. She had sailed from Port Lincoln four days before the *Archibald Russell* and there was, as one would expect, some rivalry between the two ships, so evenly matched as they were. Neither ship sighted the other on the run to Cape Horn, but they fell in with each other in the Atlantic in the vicinity of the Equator,[3] and again off the Irish coast while the *Archibald Russell* spent a further eight days beating about and made Queenstown on May 12th, having taken 124 days over her passage.

The *Hougomont* was 120 days on passage and went on to London, and the *Archibald Russell* to Antwerp.

On her next voyage she was chartered to load timber for Melbourne at a freight of 97/6 per standard.* With cargoes outward and homeward she was now making a fair profit for her owner. Part of her cargo was loaded at the Swedish port of Örnsköldsvik and on July 19th, she sailed 120 miles down the coast to Hudiksvall where the balance, which included as usual a substantial deck cargo, was loaded. With everything lashed down for the long voyage south she put to sea on August 6th, 1927. The outward passage was made round the north of Scotland, a course which her owner preferred his Masters to take because of the risk of collision while beating around in the confined waters of the English Channel.

The *Archibald Russell* was reported off the Hebrides on September 7th, and while she sailed serenely on the *Hougomont*, whose bad luck seemed to follow her under the Erikson flag as it had under Hardies, was in trouble again. Under the command of a new Captain, she had also loaded a timber cargo in Sweden and sailed from Gävle on July 25th. The next we hear of her is that, after meeting bad weather in the Bay of Biscay, she was towed into Lisbon on October 27th, 1927, with sails in tatters and her masts and rigging damaged. This could have been serious, for any extensive injury to a sailing ship's masts in these hard times meant the end of her career if excessive costs were involved, especially in Captain Erikson's fleet which sailed without insurance. The dismasting was expensive. The fore and main topgallants, which were of wood, snapped off at the topmast caps, while the damage to the mizzen was more serious, as the steel topmast broke just above the lower mast caps. Altogether, with a jigger topmast broken as well, the rigging was a tangled mass of ropes, wires and broken spars, leaving her quite unable to make port under her remaining sails. After being towed to Lisbon her Master, Captain E.H. Jansen, set about getting the *Hougomont* re-rigged, as much of the work as possible being done by the crew to keep down expenses. The job took a month to complete and cost Captain Erikson £1,400.[4] She was then able to continue her voyage. She arrived in Melbourne on March 3rd, 96 days from Lisbon, a fortnight after the *Archibald Russell* had sailed for home.

Meanwhile the *Archibald Russell* had arrived in Melbourne on December 2nd, after a passage of 118 days. On January 23rd, 1928, with her tim-

---

*A standard of sawn timber weighs approximately 3½ tons.

Plate 47 The Hougomont *dismasted, 1927. On the mizzen mast.*
H.F. Meadows

ber cargo discharged, she shifted over to Geelong to load 3,830 tons of wheat for the United Kingdom at a freight of 26/3 per ton, a very poor rate compared to the previous year.

Over in Adelaide, the *Killoran* was also discharging a timber cargo. She came from Sweden in better time than the *Archibald Russell*, having made it in 114 days. She had been busy since her purchase by Captain Erikson and had some adventures while tramping the globe, much of the time in ballast, in search of cargoes. Her first voyage in 1924 under the Erikson flag was outward in ballast to Antofagasta and home again to Garston with nitrate. Her Master during the early days with her new owner was Captain K.J. Eriksson. When sailing from the Mersey at Eastertime, 1925, she was caught in a gale before she got very far and forced to run for shelter to the Clyde with her cargo shifted; she also lost some sails. After a few days putting things to rights, she continued her voyage to Restigouche in New Brunswick, arriving 36 days from the Tail of the Bank. With her coal cargo discharged, she took on ballast and set sail for Port Lincoln, where her owner hoped to fix her homewards with wheat. She reached an anchorage off Port Lincoln on February 10th, 1926, but no wheat cargo was available so, after waiting three days, she weighed anchor and sailed round the coast to Newcastle, N.S.W. where she loaded coal for Callao, one of the last coal cargoes carried by a sailing ship from Australia to the West Coast, a trade which in the past had employed so many vessels like the *Killoran*.

Her course on what turned out to be a very long tramping voyage took her down into the stormy waters of the Southern Ocean where she nearly met her end when, during a bout of bad weather, she was pooped by a heavy sea which swept the helmsman overboard, smashed the wheel and threw the ship on her beam ends. In the middle of this catastrophe, the cargo shifted and some of her sails were blown to shreds. She was now in extreme danger, but somehow Captain Eriksson and his crew managed to trim the cargo, bring the ship back on an even keel, bend new sails and continue the voyage to Callao where she finally arrived on January 10th, 1926, 71 days from Newcastle. Neither nitrate nor guano was forthcoming, so after discharging her coal she sailed for Port Lincoln to join the grain fleet, taking 108 days, a long time for a trade wind passage across the Pacific. Then followed another long, tedious passage homeward with wheat. Two years' growth of weed and barnacles below her waterline did not help and she was 147 days to Falmouth. Now, in the January of 1928, after a passage out from Sweden with timber of 114 days, she was looking for a homeward cargo. This she got, but first she had to make a ballast passage to the guano islands of Peru to obtain it.

But returning to the *Archibald Russell*, her homeward passage was an unfortunate one. She normally was a ship which voyaged without serious incidents and was never at any time considered unlucky. She sailed from Geelong on February 21st, 1928, and everything went well on the run down to the Horn where, on the 53rd day, she encountered very heavy weather. Sail was being reduced and two men were sent out on the bowsprit to stow the inner jib and foretopmast staysail. She was running hard at the time, dipping her jibboom low over the water, when she shipped a heavy sea which swept the full length of the ship. When she cleared herself, the two men were seen in the water; although ropes were thrown to them, they had no chance with the ship sailing at twelve knots and they were soon left astern. The sea was too heavy at the time for the ship to be hove to and a boat launched, and they had to be left to their fate.

Only those who have experienced a loss amongst their shipmates can understand the feelings of the crew in such a position. In the trade under sail, the wages were low and the risks many and they all shared the common endeavour to get the ship from one end of the world to the other and back again, with little visible reward. And yet there was never a shortage of youths coming forward for such a voyage, although experienced seamen were a rarity. The loss of these two men hung like a shadow over the ship for weeks and their weight at brace and halliard was missed in a ship which was not in any sense over-manned.

The *Archibald Russell* was 119 days on passage, arriving at Queenstown on June 19th, 1928. She discharged her wheat at the South Wales port of Barry.

Chapter XV

Captain Karl Sjögren

Karl Gerhard Sjögren, the *Archibald Russell*'s First Mate, was promoted Master. Like most of Captain Erikson's Masters, he was an experienced and competent seaman. At the age of seventeen, he was shipwrecked while serving on the *California*; half of the crew perished in a storm when the barque, in ballast condition, lost contact with her tug and was driven ashore on the Yorkshire coast. Karl succeeded in swimming through the surf to safety, thanks to his strength. This episode did not deter him from continuing his career in sail. He was thirty-three when he took command of the *Archibald Russell* and knew how to get the best out of both the ship and her crew. He knew her well, having joined her in 1924 in Milford Haven.

Freight for the Erikson fleet was falling, but the ships were found cargoes, although they had to tramp all over the world to procure them. These were now confined to timber and wheat with occasional coal or guano cargoes. As far as the *Archibald Russell* was concerned, from 1926 to 1939 she traded continuously between north European ports and Australia with the regularity of a wool clipper, if not with the same speed.

From Barry she sailed to Sundsvall, arriving on August 13th. She loaded part of her timber cargo and then sailed for Larvik at the entrance to Oslo Fiord to complete. The freight was 70/- per standard, considerably less than the previous year. She sailed from Larvik on October 13th, 1928, and Captain Sjögren shaped a course round the north of Scotland. Soon after leaving the Baltic a sail was seen astern, steadily coming up. The overtaking vessel turned out to be the *Herzogin Cecilie*, with Reuben de Cloux still in command. She was in ballast condition while the *Archibald Russell* was deep loaded and encumbered with her deck cargo. They were soon within hailing distance and, for a short period, the two vessels sailed yardarm to yardarm, only a few feet apart while the crews not only exchanged greetings but were able to throw across newspapers. The *Herzogin Cecilie* quickly left the loaded vessel astern, but shortly after parting she encountered a violent gale off the north coast of Scotland. Her ballast shifted and the crew spent several days down in the hold shovelling it into place again in order to bring her back on an even keel. They survived the ordeal with nothing worse than the loss of a few sails and smashed boats. In spite of all this they made a passage of 90 days to Port Lincoln.[1]

Plate 48   Captain Karl Gerhard Sjögren
John Hackman

145

The *Archibald Russell* suffered no such incident and arrived at Melbourne on January 15th, 1929, 94 days out. Altogether she lay seven weeks in Melbourne while the timber was discharged. She was then towed to Williamstown where 3,840 tons of wheat were loaded. The freight was 32/6 per ton which was a profitable one as long as there were no unforeseen expenses incurred on the homeward passage. Also in Melbourne at this time was the four-masted barque *Garthpool*, one of the last of the limejuicers to fly the Red Ensign. She had come out from Belfast in 91 days and this was to be her final voyage before being wrecked.

The *Archibald Russell* was towed from Williamstown on Saturday, March 4th, 1929. The crew numbered only twenty-two, so few in numbers as to promise a hard time ahead of them. None the less, it turned out quite a remarkable passage. The run down to the Horn was an exceptional one, in fact the fastest achieved by any Erikson ship up to that time. She passed Cape Horn on April 1st in the morning watch during a severe storm which gave them a final great push, achieving the time of 31 days from Williamstown.[2] From the Horn on it seemed as if they might make a record passage home, faster than the *Herzogin Cecilie*'s 96 days in 1928, but unwanted days of calm in the horse latitudes frustrated this and the passage dragged out. However, the wind picked up as she neared the Western Isles and she made a glorious approach to Queenstown, overtaking the barque *Penang* and the barquentine *Mozart* on the day before making port on June 5th, 1929, 93 days out. There was great jubilation when the crew learned after anchoring that they had won the 'Grain Race' as it had become known over the years, and also that they had beaten the *Herzogin Cecilie* by six days. They were particularly pleased over this as she had the reputation of being the fastest ship in the fleet.

Soon after this, the *Archibald Russell* left for Cardiff to discharge. On July 11th, she sailed for Mariehamn and thence to the Swedish ports of Hernösand and Kramfors. At these last two ports she loaded 1,002 standards of timber at 87/6 per standard, and finally made sail for Adelaide on August 22nd, 1929, making port 110 days out on January 10th, 1930. She made a sorry picture as she lay there discharging. Her topsides were streaked with rust and she did not look at all trim aloft, with her main-topgallant mast on deck. Nor did the awning draped untidily over the poop give that cool impression which an awning should. She appeared neglected and run-down.

Freights were bad this year and cargoes few. Ships came to Australia hoping for cargoes. Some departed empty, tramping around for anything profitable. Others returned home in ballast. The unluckiest remained with-

Plate 49 The Archibald Russell *at Melbourne, 1929.*
The hulk of the Dorothy H. Sterling *in background.*
Len Williams

out any hope, their owners selling them as coal hulks or simply abandoning them when no buyer could be found. Just ahead of the *Archibald Russell* lay the American barquentine *Dorothy H. Sterling*. She was in poor shape, being dismasted for conversion to a hulk. She came in with a cargo of timber but the voyage had bankrupted her owner. The Captain and Mate had departed, leaving her in the possession of the Second Mate and a few hands who were offering the ship for sale for £500 in order to clear their wages.

Captain Erikson had, at this time, gathered a fleet of twenty-one sailing ships of different sizes and rig and the continued existence of his big, deep-water vessels depended on the Australian grain harvest and the demand for cereal in Europe. In the past three years, the *Killoran* had managed to secure only one grain cargo and during this time, made nine long passages of which five were in ballast. Her Master, Captain R. Lindholm, of whom we shall hear more later, took command in 1927 and remained until 1930. His passages in the *Killoran* were as follows:

147

1928	Adelaide to Ilo (for orders) in ballast	46 days
	Don Martin Island to London	
	with guano via the Panama Canal	91 days*
1929	London to Port Lincoln in ballast	104 days
	Port Lincoln to Ilo (for orders) in ballast again	53 days
	Santa Rosa Island to Antwerp	
	with guano via the Panama Canal	77 days
1930	Newport (Mon) to Puerto Cabello (Venezuela)	
	with patent fuel	45 days

On the coastal trip from Antwerp to Newport where she was chartered to load the patent fuel for Cabello, a cargo which consisted of coal dust compressed into brick shapes, she had difficulty in getting down the English Channel. Perhaps she was insufficiently ballasted for the short passage, but anyway adverse winds and gales forced her to anchor in the Downs on November 23rd. After a week of delay at anchor and no change in the weather, she was taken in tow, getting as far as the Isle of Wight before the gales forced her to shelter in St Helen's Roads where she remained while the winds raged and did not pass the Lizard until December 16th, arriving at Newport next day, 26 days in all for the 600-mile passage from Antwerp.

On January 12th, with her cargo aboard, she towed out of Newport and anchored in Barry Roads waiting for a fair wind. When she finally got away, there was concern for her safety on account of a report from the German steamship *Fasolt* that she had sighted one of the *Killoran*'s lifeboats in 39°33′N, 9°44′W, waterlogged and empty. In fact she had taken a beating in heavy weather during which the lifeboat was washed overboard and two members of the crew with it, but the ship herself was safe and sound.

She sailed from Puerto Cabello on April 25th, arriving at Falmouth 43 days later. Her next voyage took her from Kotka in Sweden to Port Lincoln in ballast to load a grain cargo homeward. After all this tramping around for cargoes, she settled down to the steady life of a grain trader for the next few years.

And what of the *Hougomont* during this period? After the damage to her masts was repaired in Lisbon, she sailed to Melbourne in 96 days from the River Tagus, arriving on March 3rd, 1928. There was no homeward cargo

---

*Arrived London in tow of tug *Java* after collision with the Italian steamship *Puerto Campanella* 25 miles south-west of Beachy Head, September 21st, 1928.

148

available so, like the *Killoran* that year, she sailed in ballast for Peru in order to load guano, making a slightly slower time of 49 days to Ilo. She loaded at Santa Rosa Island and then set sail for Jacksonville in Florida via the Panama Canal. There was no timber or coal cargo for her there, so it was back in ballast to South Australia where she arrived off Port Lincoln on February 21st, 1929, 104 days out from Jacksonville, in the hope of obtaining a grain cargo. This was 1929, with more wheat around for transhipment. She loaded her cargo at Port Lincoln and by April 3rd, was on her way, making a passage of 117 days to Queenstown, where she was ordered to Avonmouth.

The passage across to Avonmouth did not go smoothly. The wind was foul in St. George's Channel and she spent four days beating against it before she passed Lundy Island, where two tugs were waiting for her. They steamed alongside, haggling with the Captain over the cost of a tow, but their offers were spurned and the *Hougomont* sailed on to Barry Roads, where she engaged the services of one of the tugs to tow her to Walton Bay, some five miles west of Avonmouth. The weather was worsening as they reached the Bay and the wind by now had increased to gale force; the pilot, Mr Cyril Hunt, advised Captain Jansen that the wind was too strong for the barque to enter the Royal Edward Dock safely, so two anchors were dropped and the *Hougomont* left to ride out the storm.

Plate 50   Coming up Channel, July 1930
National Maritime Museum

149

Plate 51 Mariehamn. The Archibald Russell *getting under weigh from the outer harbour, September 1930. The* Viking *anchored beyond.*

National Maritime Museum

There is no shelter in Walton Bay from winds anywhere north of west and east and soon the *Hougomont*, yawing and plunging at her cables, started to drag towards the Welsh Grounds. Flares were fired for tugs which steamed down from Avonmouth to tow her back to deeper water. However, there was no let-up in the storm which continued unabated for 48 hours, during which the *Hougomont* again dragged her anchors and had to call on the tugs for a second tow. Each time this happened, the crew had to man the capstan and heave home 800 ft of cable on each anchor, which took a long time and entailed much back-breaking work at the capstan as for some reason the donkey-boiler and engine were not used.[3] Perhaps they were short of coal. On August 2nd, the day dawned fine and sunny and much to the relief of Captain Jansen and Cyril Hunt, the *Hougomont* was towed into Avonmouth and berthed at 'V' shed on the Eastern Arm Extension of the Royal Edward Dock.[4]

1930 turned out to be another lean year for the grain fleet, with only a handful of the Erikson ships obtaining a wheat charter homeward, and this year we find the *Hougomont* about to sail from Avonmouth on another of those world-encircling voyages in search of cargoes. With nothing offering in Europe, she loaded 1,500 tons of sand ballast and was soon on her way

150

to Australia; by the New Year of 1930, she was in Port Pirie loading wheat for Callao. She was 71 days to Callao and then went on to Vancouver to load a timber cargo which she brought to Durban, arriving on December 28th, 1930, 142 days out. She then went on to Port Lincoln in ballast and home with wheat to Falmouth in 139. She received orders from London and arrived in the Thames on December 26th, 1931.

On the Vancouver/Durban leg of the voyage, an Irish poet named Shaw Desmond took passage in her. He was a somewhat eccentric man in his forties. He was treated throughout by the Captain and officers as an honoured guest and it was Captain Erikson's specific wish that they should do so. The *Hougomont*, whose bottom was rather foul, was slow and unhandy at times on the passage round Cape Horn. Shaw Desmond kept a diary, published later, in which he gave a studied account in great detail of the ship and her crew. He himself was a romantic and wrote in a poetic way, as one would expect, about the pains and pleasures of sail, but at the same time he did not gloss over the bickering that went on, the squalor and the harshness of life at the tail end of the large, deep-water sailing ship era. His picture of the Master, Captain Sandström, was of a large, rather overweight person who went unshaven for a week at a time, wore shirts with no collars and shoes with no laces; but apart from these little habits, he considered him to be one of nature's gentlemen and an excellent seaman.[5] It was just as well that Shaw Desmond didn't stay to complete the voyage back to England, as it proved to be a very worrying one with bad weather round the Horn, during which the *Hougomont* sprang a leak, keeping the crew busy at the pumps. But we are ahead of ourselves here.

As already mentioned, it was a lean year in Australia. Only eight ships obtained wheat cargoes from the Spencer Gulf in 1930 and the *Archibald Russell* was one of the fortunate ones. After taking on ballast, she sailed from Adelaide to Port Lincoln where she loaded 3,836 tons of wheat at 22/-. She set sail for the United Kingdom on March 15th and was 43 days to Cape Horn, making Queenstown on July 2nd, after a passage of 110 days. Three days before she arrived, the weather main-topgallant brace parted in a heavy squall, the sail being lost and others split. Apart from this, the voyage was uneventful. After six days in Queenstown, she received orders for London and left on the 8th, arriving four days later on the 12th. She berthed in Millwall Dock, where she had a quick discharge and twelve days later, on July 24th, she was on her way to Mariehamn, where she anchored in the Sound on August 4th. Captain Sjögren left her there to take command of the *Pamir*, his place being taken by Captain Harald Lindfors.

Chapter XVI

Captain Harald Lindfors

Captain Lindfors was only twenty-five at the time of joining the *Archibald Russell*. Previously, he had been several years in the *Herzogin Cecilie*, first as a seaman before the mast and later rising to become her First Mate. In 1930, Captain Erikson gave him command of the *Carmen*, a pretty little white-painted barque with old-fashioned turned stanchions around the poop. He sailed in her for a season after which he came to the *Archibald Russell*. The First Mate was J. Frederiksson and the Second Mate Paul Sommarlund, who eventually rose to command the *Archibald Russell*. Raoul Rasmussen, a young Finnish seaman, joined in Mariehamn on his first deep-water voyage. Although only fifteen at the time, he had already served on a coasting schooner. He wrote that he considered the *Archibald Russell* to be a good ship, one of the best in his opinion, with a good Captain and officers and a congenial crew.[1]

After sailing from Mariehamn, her first call was Copenhagen, where she took on the last of her stores for the voyage. On September 19th, 1930, she set sail for Australia. Captain Lindfors decided to take the northerly route and the first few days were fine with smooth sailing. Off the coast of Scotland, however, the weather changed and they were lashed by a storm which caused the ballast to shift and the crew spent two days down in the hold re-stowing it in order to get her back on an even keel. After this they had no more problems and Port Lincoln was reached on December 21st, 93 days from Copenhagen. Freights were higher in 1931 and she secured a cargo at 33/9 per ton, which was a profitable rate in spite of the outward passage in ballast. She loaded 48,233 bags of wheat with a gross freight of £6,481.19/- and sailed on January 26th, 1931. They encountered heavy weather in the Roaring Forties, being frequently reduced to short canvas while the decks were swept by heavy seas. Raoul Rasmussen remembered seeing seven icebergs off Cape Horn, a hazard which could always be expected in summertime in the southern seas. She came to Falmouth in 98 days. The only other vessel this year to make a better passage than the *Archibald Russell* was the *Herzogin Cecilie*, which was 93 days from Wallaroo. She was again ordered to London to discharge and sailed for Mariehamn on June 10th, arriving nine days later on June 19th, 1931.

The next voyage did not go so smoothly. This year the owner had been fortunate to obtain a timber cargo for South Africa and the *Archibald Rus-*

152

Plate 52   At the Royal Victoria Dock, London, 1931
National Maritime Museum

153

Plate 53 The Archibald Russell *photographed from the* Graf Zeppelin
Captain Hugo Eckener

sell sailed from Mariehamn for the Swedish port of Kotka. Although this was only a short distance, she had been insufficiently ballasted and she would not stay. The passage was protracted due to gales and fog. The bad weather continued during the loading and as a result there was further delay. It was August 7th before she was ready for sea. Complete with deck cargo, she set sail from Kotka bound for East London and was immediately buffeted by storms, at times being reduced to topsails, as she beat back and forth between Sweden and the Danish coast on her way to Copenhagen, where she rested for a while to take on stores, sailing on August 20th. Six days later she was reported passing Dover.

Eighteen days out, all was going well with the ship bowling along on the starboard tack with a great bone in her teeth. On that day, with Madeira just beyond the horizon, a strange object was sighted coming towards them, which proved to be the airship *Graf Zeppelin*, outward bound to Buenos Aires. Her commander, Captain Hugo Eckener, took a fine picture of the *Archibald Russell* from a height of two or three hundred feet. The ships exchanged greetings and passed on their way. The *Archibald Russell* reached East London on November 8th, 1931, after a passage of 80 days.

After ten days in East London discharging part of the timber, she sailed

154

for Lourenço Marques on November 18th to discharge the remainder. The passage up the coast was a stormy one. The distance was only 550 miles but it took her fourteen days' hard struggle against the Agulhas Current before she made port.

After the cargo was discharged, the *Archibald Russell* loaded ballast and sailed for the Spencer Gulf on December 22nd. Now began a long battle to make an offing and clear the African coast. Captain Lindfors was anxious to sail south and east towards the Roaring Forties which would give him a fair wind to Australia, but the wind remained stubbornly in the east, blowing at gale force. Being in ballast, he found the ship setting towards a lee shore, which was too close for comfort. Sail was crowded on in order to make headway and Christmas Day was spent with no respite. To add to the Captain's troubles the steward, cook, Third Mate and donkeyman were all laid up with some sort of sickness. The struggle lasted for eight days, during which the gaff topsail and the fore and mizzen lower topgallant sails were lost. At one time, he was forced to anchor and avoid being set ashore. Finally on New Year's Eve, much to everyone's relief, with the wind in a favourable quarter at last, they left the coast of Africa behind

Plate 54 The Port Watch. Raoul Rasmussen third from left. On extreme right, Paul Sommarlund, later Captain of the Archibald Russell.
R. Rasmussen

155

Plate 55   Sailing up the Spencer Gulf, 1932
M.R. Phillips

and ran down to Port Lincoln in 36 days, arriving on January 27th ,1932. Much of the ballast was discharged there and on February 5th, the anchor was weighed and the ship sailed under easy canvas across the Gulf to the little port of Wallaroo on the eastern side, where she was chartered to load a full cargo of wheat at 31/6 per ton.

Wallaroo's sturdy jetty could accommodate several ships safely, although at times they surged uncomfortably at their moorings during strong winds. The wheat was transported from the mainland in rail trucks, which trundled down the half-mile long jetty to the ships, where the bags were loaded by means of chutes into the holds of the waiting sailers. The people of Wallaroo were friendly, and tolerant of the high-spirited excesses of the seamen. Their hospitality was sometimes returned by dances held on board the ships in the cool of the evening, the decks full of dancers under the lofty spars. Many a romantic attachment was formed between the sailors and local girls. Desertions were not uncommon as a result.

Loading was a leisurely affair. After a quantity of wheat was loaded for stiffening, the *Archibald Russell* was moved under sail to the ballast grounds to discharge the remaining ballast. It was shovelled into baskets, lifted from the holds by means of the donkey engine and dumped overboard. It was hard work for the crew in the extreme heat of the Australian summer. When the wind favoured, sail was made back to the jetty to complete loading.

Meanwhile the *Killoran*, which we last heard of in 1930, had reached the Spencer Gulf on March 15th, 1931, 44 days out from Lourenço Marques. She then sailed home with her cargo of wheat in 120 days to Falmouth. After discharging in London, she sailed for Port Lincoln, arriving on December 14th, 1931, 86 days out. She loaded her wheat at Port Augusta and was away homeward on January 21st, before either the *Archibald Russell* or the *Hougomont* had reached Australia. Everything was going fine for her. But not so for the *Hougomont*, which was having difficulty in getting away from the Channel and was heading for disaster.

Captain Sandström, he who had the poet Shaw Desmond with him on the *Hougomont*, left after his long tramping voyage, his place being taken by Captain Lindholm who it will be remembered was previously master of the *Killoran*. The First Mate was Alexander Backman.[2] The *Hougomont* left Gravesend under tow on the last day of December, 1931. She had no cargo, only 1,200 tons of ballast aboard, but the wind was fair and the crew hoped for a good passage down Channel. However, the setting out commenced badly. Before they reached Beachy Head, the wind turned against them, increasing to gale force and, although they made tacks back

Plate 56   Wheat stacks at Port Augusta, South Australia
R. Mayes

and forth across the Channel they were unable to make headway. Later the wind dropped and fog came down. During the gale several sails had been lost and these had to be replaced between frequent bouts of tacking, no mean task with a new crew. Into the bargain, they were in continual danger of being run down by passing steamers. Captain Lindholm decided to turn back for Dover and wait for a favourable slant of wind.

For the next 30 days, during which time they went unreported, they were driven about the North Sea by a series of gales, with sails blown out quicker than they could repair them and it was January 31st before the wind came from the north, enabling them to set a course for Dover, which they passed on February 1st, after a battle of 33 days over a passage which might have been expected to take 24 hours. All hands, with hardly any sleep, were worn out with the continual work at brace and halliard and replacement of torn sails. On February 2nd, they passed Dover, requesting to be reported to the owner, who must have been wondering what the ship had been doing all this time when she should have been near the Equator. However, from then on she made good time and by April 19th, they were only 700 miles from Port Victoria and 77 days out from the second westward passing of Dover, which must be considered good time. In the Roaring Forties, a day's run of over 300 miles was recorded.

All this suddenly came to an end in the early hours of April 20th. During the previous day, the wind and sea had been moderate and the *Hougomont* carried all sail except royals, which were furled. The barometer was low but steady and when the Master retired for the night, he left orders for sail to be reduced at the first sign of a fall in pressure.

When Mr Backman went down to his cabin for his watch below, he had barely been asleep for twenty minutes when he was aroused by an apprentice shouting through his doorway. 'Mr Mate, the foremast has gone overboard.' A few seconds later he returned shouting, 'Mr Mate, the main-mast and the mizzen topgallants have gone too.' Mr Backman couldn't believe it, but it was true. In fact, when disaster overcame the ship, four seamen were aloft on the foremast when a black squall struck them with wind speed estimated at over 90 m.p.h. The rigging was unable to withstand the blast and the fore-topgallant and topmast came down to

Plate 57   After the squall. The Hougomont's *luck runs out.*
National Maritime Museum

159

starboard, bringing with them the complete mainmast and also the topgallant mast and yards of the mizzen. The four men aloft at the time on the foremast managed to get down on deck, an almost miraculous escape considering the speed with which the intricate structure of the masts and rigging collapsed. In the pitch black of the night, it was hard to ascertain the extent of the damage. Much of the gear was still aloft, swinging about as the ship rolled in the rising sea, a constant danger to all those at work around the decks. The spars in the water battered themselves against the ship's side, threatening at any moment to put a hole in her. Only one lifeboat remained undamaged and this was prepared for launching.

However, abandoning ship was not yet considered by Captain Lindholm. He ordered the crew to set about cutting the stays to free the ship of the spars, since it was beyond their ability to save them. The seas were now running at a height of 25 to 30 ft, the crests crashing down over the decks, while the *Hougomont* rolled violently, adding greatly to the difficulty of the work. The crew, using axes, chisels and saws, attacked the stays of which there were several dozen of steel wire ranging from 2 to 4^1_2 ins in circumference. Some time during the day, while they hacked and hewed at the rigging, the heavy rolling finally brought down the mizzen topmast and yards, but by 10 pm, the ship was freed of all the wreckage. They lay the rest of the night in comparative safety but the ship, with no sail to steady her, continued to roll so heavily that the sand ballast was in danger of shifting.

Daylight revealed a sorry spectacle. Of the masts, only the fore, mizzen and jigger lower masts were standing, and all the spars were gone save the broken fore-yard and the crossjack, cockbilled and useless. In spite of all this, Captain Lindholm decided to try and sail the remaining distance to the nearest port and accordingly, they set about hoisting sails wherever possible; the jigger topsail was set on the forestay and a spare royal yard and sail was hoisted at the fore lowermast; to this motley pair was added a small staysail on the jigger mast, and with this makeshift rig they set a course for the Spencer Gulf. Fortunately the winds were mainly favourable from the westward, but at one period the wind went north-east blowing them away from their goal. After 17 days, during which time several vessels approached them offering help, they finally dropped anchor in Adelaide Roads, having by their own efforts saved Captain Erikson any salvage claims against the ship. Altogether it was a very creditable achievement by the Master, officers and crew, a feat equal to that of the *Dallam Tower* half a century earlier.

However, it was the end for the old *Hougomont*. It has been suggested that the dismasting was caused by the corrosion at the heel of the foremast

Plate 58 The Archibald Russell *sailing from Wallaroo, 1932*
A.D. Edwardes Collection, State Library of South Australia

which, having subsided slightly, caused the rigging to go slack, setting up a chain of reaction with the other masts. Captain Erikson did not consider that it was a viable proposition to re-rig her and she was offered for sale as she lay, for a coal hulk or some other humble purpose.

*   *   *   *   *   *   *

Back in Wallaroo, the *Archibald Russell* had completed loading and sailed for the United Kingdom on March 12th, 1932. Captain Lindfors' bad luck still dogged him. She was 50 days to the Horn, experiencing much dirty weather on the way. April 5th was a particularly hectic day when the gale reached hurricane force, catching the *Archibald Russell* and four other vessels in the vicinity making for the Horn. With so few sailing ships in commission, it was strange that five four-masted barques were battling for their lives in the same storm not far from each other. One of them was the Swedish training vessel *C.B. Pedersen*, which was so severely damaged aloft she had to run north away from these stormy latitudes and continue her voyage home through the Panama Canal. The large Finnish four-masted barque *Parma* was pooped and consequently

161

broached to, being very nearly lost.[3] Three other Finns, the *Pamir*, the *Pommern* and the *Melbourne* also got the brunt of the storm. The *Pamir* lost her spanker boom and was flooded out in the after accommodation, the *Pommern* lost some sails and the *Melbourne* sustained damage to her deckhouse. The *Melbourne* was unfortunately to be sunk in collision several weeks later off the Irish Coast with heavy loss of life. As for the *Archibald Russell*, at the height of the storm the port watch, while working at the braces, was caught by a heavy sea breaking aboard which washed them around the decks and into the scuppers. Fortunately no-one went overboard but the Mate, Mr. Frederikson, and the Third Mate were caught under a spare spar, the Mate breaking both his legs and the Third Mate his hip. Captain Lindfors, with the help of the Second Mate, set the broken limbs in the saloon under conditions of great difficulty, with the ship rolling violently under the onslaught of the seas.

The southern latitudes around Cape Horn are about the most desolate in the world. The few vessels which still sailed this route rarely sighted one another. These lonely ships existed in a world of their own, fighting their

Plate 59 The Archibald Russell *in her new colours getting under way,*
September 1932
National Maritime Museum

162

battle for survival in the knowledge that no help would be forthcoming if they lost. In time of trouble, since few sailing vessels carried radio, any contact was visual and purely by chance. The awareness of this isolation gave the crews a sense of unity stronger than that of other men thrown together. The safety of the ship depended on the efforts of the highest and the lowest on board. The large sailing ship was at times a hazardous means of transport. A ship running before a strong gale, with great seas roaring up astern, was virtually out of control as she yawed on either side of her intended course with the helmsman struggling to keep her steady. The loss of a sail, a brace parting or even the snuffing out of the binnacle light, could mean disaster.

The *Archibald Russell* survived the storm, making her way south of the Falkland Islands and up into the Atlantic, where the North-East Trades carried her steadily homewards. In the North Atlantic, she was plagued by calms and adverse winds and the voyage became so protracted that she ran short of fuel and food, having to beg from a passing steamer. She reached Falmouth on July 26th, 1932, after a dismal passage of 136 days during which she had been becalmed for 24 days in the North Atlantic.

Plate 60   Derelict. The hulk of the Hougomont.
A.D. Edwardes Collection, State Library of South Australia

Plate 61 Wallaroo, 1932. The Archibald Russell *in company with the*
Abraham Rydberg *and the* Penang.
The Advertiser, *Adelaide.*

She proceeded to London where her cargo was discharged. Later she moved
to East Thurrock to load her ballast. While waiting to dock, she was moored to
buoys in company with the four-masted barque *Olivebank*. The crew were put
to work painting the hull and when she sailed on her next voyage, her colour
scheme had been changed from white to black. Captain Lindfors left the ship
in London, his place being taken by Captain Werner Öjst.

This year she did not make her usual visit to Mariehamn. After taking in
ballast she sailed from the Thames on September 4th, and on the following
day she was in trouble off the Goodwins. While making her way through
the Straits of Dover, she was forced by contrary winds to anchor perilously
close to the Goodwin Sands, a very worrying situation for her new Captain,
but her luck held and she was soon able to continue on her way, making
Port Lincoln in 92 days on December 15th, 1932. Orders were received to
proceed to Wallaroo, where she was chartered to load a cargo of wheat at a
freight of 27/3 per ton, considerably less than the previous cargo.

The hulk of the *Hougomont* was still around, waiting for disposal. There was much useful gear on board which could be used on other sailing ships of the Erikson fleet. This year, before sailing homeward, Erikson's *Herzogin Cecilie* manoeuvered alongside her and lifted out all the spare sails, spars, ropes, winches, the charthouse and wheel shelter, all of which were to be discharged in Mariehamn on arrival. No-one came forward to purchase the *Hougomont*, not even for use as a coal hulk, neither did she have any scrap value in Australia at that time. In the end she was given away, virtually for nothing, and on January 7th, 1933, with Captain Lindholm still in command, she was towed to Stenhouse Bay on the Yorke Peninsula, where she was sunk to act as a breakwater for a jetty.[4]

Wallaroo was busy in the New Year of 1933. Loading at the jetty with the *Archibald Russell* were two other sailing vessels, the Swedish training ship *Abraham Rydberg* and the barque *Penang*. There were also three large steamers at the jetty. However, loading went quite quickly; by January 9th, she was ready for sea and together with the *Abraham Rydberg* she sailed on that day. They parted company when they cleared the Spencer Gulf, the *Abraham Rydberg* taking the easier route round the Cape of Good Hope while the *Archibald Russell* turned east for the Horn. She encountered very heavy weather in which some of the crew were injured. A few days later, when off the Falkland Islands, she was caught by a violent squall and before sail could be shortened, ten of them were badly torn or completely blown out of their bolt ropes.

She was 119 days to Falmouth, where she arrived on May 8th. She received orders for Ipswich and, on her way to Harwich while under tow, a passing steamer caused her to take a sheer and before the tug could straighten her, she ran aground. She was later towed off by the Trinity House tender *Alert* on the following tide, fortunately without any damage. From Harwich she sailed for Mariehamn. She was now twenty-eight years old and due for reclassification. Considerable work was carried out on her rigging and some of her yards were sent down on deck for repairs.

Towards the end of September, the *Archibald Russell* sailed for Copenhagen, where she was drydocked.

Chapter XVII

Captain Mikael Sjögren

Captain Mikael Sjögren, who had been the First Mate on the previous voyage, took command of the *Archibald Russell* in the autumn of 1933. He was the younger brother of Karl Sjögren. He was a large man known in the Erikson fleet as 'Big Mike' and a seaman to his fingertips. He started his career at sixteen, just after the Great War, first sailing in Baltic ketches and schooners and later graduating to deep-water ships, where he sailed before the mast in the *Mozart*, the *Bellhouse* and others. He was three years as Chief Mate of the barque *Penang* and, after obtaining his Master's Certificate, he came to the *Archibald Russell*. He was completely fearless, driving the ship to her limit when possible. He did not succeed in making any exceptional homeward passages in her, although some of his outward ones were creditable. However, he kept her out of trouble all the time he was in her. Later, when in command of Erikson's huge four-masted barque *Moshulu*, which was a stronger, more powerful ship, he showed he could get the most out of a vessel by doing some spectacular sailing, bringing her home from the Spencer Gulf in 1939 in 91 days, the fastest passage of the year. Several men who sailed with him recorded their impressions. He seemed to be well liked and respected, perhaps sometimes feared, since he did not hesitate to use his fists when necessary to maintain discipline. He had a great sense of humour. When sail was finished, he continued his career in steamships and died in 1975 at the age of seventy-three years.

On October 3rd, 1933, the *Archibald Russell* passed the Skaw outward bound for the Spencer Gulf. There was no timber cargo for her this year. Captain Sjögren brought the ship to anchor off Port Victoria, 94 days from the Skaw. This year two German four-masted barques, the *Priwall* and the *Padua*, joined the grain fleet. They sailed from Hamburg to the Spencer Gulf in 65 days, just about the smartest piece of sailing of the twentieth century. In all fairness to the ships of the Erikson fleet, the German ships were manned by a large number of cadets, having crews over twice the size of the Finnish vessels.

The *Archibald Russell* was seven weeks discharging her ballast and loading her cargo consisting of 3,827 tons of wheat at a freight of only 25/6 per ton. Colin Heggie of Adelaide, with ambitions to see the world, sailed in the *Archibald Russell* on this homeward passage. Like so many Australian youths with the call of the sea in them, he gave his muscle and

Plate 62   The end of a long jetty.
The four-masted barque Abraham Rydberg *at Wallaroo*
M. Marsh

enthusiasm for little or nothing, but he enjoyed the life. On Friday, February 15th, 1934, the wind being fair, the anchor was weighed and sail made for the voyage to Falmouth. Full of the romance of youth, Colin noted in his diary the beauty of the sunrise over Kangaroo Island as they sailed out of the Spencer Gulf. Captain Sjögren, assessing the weather as settled, decided to make use of the easterly wind and try for the easier passage to the westward via the Cape of Good Hope. All went well for a few days and they made good time, but on February 26th, the wind came out of the west at gale force and they were soon reduced to lower topsails, struggling to make westing. There was some talk of turning and running for the Horn. However, on February 28th, 12 days out, they managed to pass Cape Leeuwin and were soon heading towards warmer weather.

On March 7th, they crossed the Tropic of Capricorn, running steadily in the trades with all sails set, scattering the flying fish before them. On the 10th the wind became light and for eight days they were virtually becalmed. The crew sweated and the pitch bubbled in the seams of the deck. Captain Sjögren was not happy with the ship's trim and during this calm spell, the crew was employed humping sacks of wheat around the hold until he was satisfied. On March 27th a sail was sighted slowly overtaking them. She proved to be the four-masted barque *Ponape* belonging to the same firm. For the next fourteen days they were never far from each other. On Easter Sunday, the two ships sailed so close that Captain Sjögren was able to shout across to Captain Granith and invite him to dinner. This meeting was especially interesting to Colin as his brother, Wally, was a seaman aboard her, doing his second voyage to England.

On April 2nd, they sighted the African coast. At that time they were under all sail, making 4 knots, when without warning the wind shifted ahead in a sudden squall, catching them flat aback. For a while, all hell was let loose and some of the crew feared the sticks would go overboard in the same manner as her sister the *Hougomont* the previous year, but with an almighty bang some of the lighter sails blew out of the boltropes to relieve the pressure. The crew worked like heroes to get the remaining sails stowed and for the next few days they were fighting head winds under short canvas.

On April 12th, she fell in with the *Ponape* for the last time until Falmouth. The crew hoped that they would not see her again, as each time she appeared, the Mates were chasing around setting sails and sweating up on brace and halliard in an effort to increase the speed, as if they didn't have enough work as it was.

They crossed the longitude of Cape Town on April 12th. 30 days later, they were off St Helena and on May 14th, 87 days out, they crossed the Equator. They were eight days becalmed in the Sargasso Sea until the wind came round from the west. On June 17th, they sighted the distant sails of *L'Avenir*, which pleased Captain Sjögren as she had sailed ten days before them. This was some comfort for a long passage, to know that they had caught her up. When they dropped anchor in Falmouth on June 26th, they were hard on the heels of the *Ponape* and both ships were 130 days out. However, the *Archibald Russell* benefited from this lengthy passage with so much fine weather, which had given the crew every opportunity to get her in good order alow and aloft, and as she lay in Falmouth Roads, she looked a picture of a well kept sailing ship. From Falmouth she sailed for Belfast to discharge and thence to Mariehamn on August 8th, arriving on the 20th where some of the *Hougomont*'s gear was transferred to the *Archibald Russell*, the sails especially being useful because the two ships were identical in size. She lay there nearly a month and on September 14th, with a new crew signed on, she sailed for the Spencer Gulf. It was 15 days before she cleared Copenhagen, making a passage of 102 days from there to Port Lincoln, arriving on January 9th, 1935. Next she was reported at Port Victoria, but finally completed loading her cargo at Port Germein.

Plate 63 L'Avenir *and* Winterhude *loading wheat on the Port Germein jetty,*
1934. The barquentine Mozart *anchored off, waiting her turn.*
The Miller Collection, State Library of South Australia

It was her first visit to this port and subsequently, apart from 1936, she
loaded every homeward cargo there. Typical of other Spencer Gulf ports,
it had a wooden jetty stretching one mile out into the Spencer Gulf, reaching southward over the shallow waters, giving the smaller deep-water sailers just sufficient draught to load their cargoes without grounding. The
township lying at the long jetty consisted of little more than a cluster of
weatherboard cottages and one hotel. However, it did have a school with
an energetic teacher who encouraged the children to compile a journal of
local events, and visiting ships played an important part in it. The few that
came made the port live for a while, brought new faces, contact with
another world and in these hard times, employment. They also marked the
passing of the seasons, coming in the high summer and departing in the
fall. The journal, which is still in existence, covered the period 1934-1940,
and the *Archibald Russell* came in for frequent mention.[1] It was recorded
that she sailed on March 21st, the last ship to load at Port Germein that
year. The dockers celebrated the occasion at a local building known as the
Institute with a cabaret show, a sort of end-of-season ritual.

Shortly after she sailed from Port Germein, one of the crew fell sick and
Captain Sjögren set a course for Port Victoria to get the services of a doc-

169

tor. On the 24th she finally cleared port and set sail for the United Kingdom. She put into Falmouth for orders on July 14th, 1935 after a passage of 111 days and then made her way round to Hull. After discharging her cargo and taking on ballast she set sail for Mariehamn, making a very protracted passage of 23 days to do the 1,000 miles from Hull. Several other vessels however took even longer.

On her next voyage to Australia, she made a smart passage of 87 days outward from the Skaw to Port Victoria. She loaded her wheat cargo there and returned home in 104 days, arriving at Falmouth on June 8th, 1936. Her cargo was discharged at Glasgow. The people of Glasgow made quite a fuss of the old ship. It was her first visit since 1915 and hundreds of people came down to see her, including the Russell family who were shown round the ship with great courtesy by the officers. From there she went to Gothenberg to refit and take on her crew.

She was 90 days from Gothenberg to the Spencer Gulf. It was noted in the Port Germein School's record of events that she loaded part of her cargo down the coast at Port Broughton, a jetty port similar to Port Germein, and on February 19th, 1937 she tied up at the Port Germein jetty to take the balance of her wheat. Her homeward passage was a fair one, 98 days, but there were several better passages that year. She discharged at the South Wales port of Barry.

Plate 64 The Archibald Russell *in Bridgwater Bay, July 1937*
J.W. Lankester, from Sea Breezes *Archives*

Plate 65   Becalmed off Dover, September 1937
National Maritime Museum

She was in her thirty-second year and once again due for reclassification, and after taking aboard sand ballast, some 800 tons of it, she went
into drydock for hull inspection, painting and fumigating, during which
they killed over 200 rats which had made their home in the hold. On July
24th, she set sail for Nystad. The passage turned out to be a tedious one.
Claude Beneke, an Australian seaman who had signed on in Falmouth,
recorded some of the problems. Captain Sjögren's wife joined in Barry
and some of the crew predictably put the blame on the lady for the subsequent bad luck which beset them.

Two tugs assisted the *Archibald Russell* from the dock and, because the
wind was from ahead, the crew expected a tow as far as Lundy Island. But
for some reason the tow was slipped before she was clear of Barry Roads
when both anchors had to be hurriedly dropped while the sails were sheet-
ed home. When she finally got under way again, there commenced a
weary beat down the Bristol Channel, tacking between the Somerset and
Welsh coasts, anchoring on the flood and making as much headway as
possible on the ebb. She cleared Lundy rounding the Longships three days
out and was reported off the Lizard soon after. The following day, July
28th, when she was off Plymouth, a seaman who had injured his hand in a

171

brace block was taken ashore to hospital by a fishing boat.

The wind continued to head them as the *Archibald Russell* beat her weary way up channel until finally a calm set in, leaving her drifting slowly onward with the flood while anchoring when the ebb set in. This progress continued for ten days until August 6th, when she was reported off Dover. Bad luck continued to dog her until August 10th, when she was involved in a collision 50 miles off the Danish coast with the fishing vessel *Thyboron* whose mast fouled the rigging and snapped. Beneke was on deck when it happened and just missed being struck by the heavy wooden mast which fell on the head of a Norwegian seaman standing alongside him. The fishermen clambered aboard to safety, shocked by the suddenness of the collision and wild with fury which was understandable, since the opinion was that the *Archibald Russell* should have given way. The fishing boat was later salvaged, but in the meantime the crew was put ashore at Esjberg.

Adverse winds and calms continued while the *Archibald Russell* drifted on, passing Elsinore on August 17th. Captain Sjögren, whose patience

Plate 66   Sailing from Mariehamn
Åland Sjofartsmuseum

172

must have been stretched to the limit by the weather conditions and the constant tacking and manoeuvering amongst heavy traffic, finally brought the ship to Nystad in the Åland Islands on September 1st, 38 days from Barry.

Captain Erikson came aboard to inspect his ship; a new fore-topgallant mast was floated out and stowed on deck to be rigged at a later date when time permitted, and then she got under weigh again for the Finnish port of Kemi, 400 miles to the north on the Arctic Circle, where she was chartered to load a timber cargo for South Africa. September 7th found her at anchor off Kemi where one might have expected her to be granted a peaceful spell, but it was not to be. Soon she was in trouble with high winds during which she dragged her anchors until she grounded firmly in shoal water, requiring three tugs to tow her clear which they succeeded in doing with some difficulty but no damage. After this episode loading went on steadily, the timber coming out on barges. Eventually, she sailed from Kemi complete with deck cargo, calling at Copenhagen on the way to pick up stores for the following voyage.[2]

Plate 67   The new fore-topgallant mast
C. Beneke

173

The voyage proper commenced on October 9th and took 87 days to Port Natal. The timber cargo stacked on deck and lashed down with chains and wires made work at the braces awkward: there were various spaces between the timber to enable the crew to get at the halliard winches and pumps and also for access to their accommodation; in the dark it was inevitable that there were a few tumbles down these traps, with severe bruising. However, according to Claude Beneke, the passage to South Africa was pleasant and uneventful until the Cape was reached, where they encountered dirty weather, losing some of the deck cargo overboard. One incident occurred in the South Atlantic when the lookout deserted his post on the fo'c'sle head in a panic, being convinced that he heard a heavenly choir singing, not the only time ghostly sounds were heard on the *Archibald Russell*. Some of the impressionable members of the crew became unsettled by this, but it was soon forgotten when they reached Port Natal. After discharging part of the cargo there, they sailed up the coast to Lourenço Marques to discharge the remainder.

She finally left the coast on February 17th, 1938, and ran to Port Lincoln in 31 days. On March 8th, while she was still many miles away, the Port Germein children recorded that she had been chartered to load at their port again and that they could expect her any day. On March 24th, she had the misfortune to lose her fore royal yard. She let go her anchor off Port Lincoln two days later and received orders to Port Germein for her wheat cargo.[3]

1938 was a busy year for the little port. Altogether, five sailing ships loaded there and from January to May, their hulls graced the scenery. They were all old friends, stragglers of a dying trade. *L'Avenir*, now flying the German ensign, had been the first to load. The rather sorry-looking barque *Winterhude* loaded next, followed by the *Killoran* and the *Pommern*. Finally, it was the *Archibald Russell*'s turn and she lay at the end of the jetty with her fore-topgallant mast on deck ready to be replaced by the new one, while 47,977 bags, comprising approximately 3,900 tons of wheat, were loaded. Her owner was paid 35/- per ton, a very profitable rate.

During these years, the *Archibald Russell* and the *Killoran* quite frequently came together. In 1934, these survivors of J. Hardie & Co. were berthed together in Belfast, discharging their wheat. There were other times when they were anchored together in the Sound of Mariehamn before going their separate ways. Did James Hardie, now in his sixties and still carrying on his business at 11, Bothwell Street, ever follow the fortunes of his old ships? Their names were always turning up in the shipping periodicals, especially as there was at this time a surge of nostalgic interest in the so-called 'Grain Race'.

Little has been said about the *Killoran*'s passages since 1930. They were in the same pattern as those of the *Archibald Russell*:

1931	Wallaroo	to	Falmouth	120 days
	London	to	Port Lincoln	86 days
1932	Port Augusta	to	Falmouth	131 days
	Elsinore	to	Port Victoria	96 days
1933	Port Victoria	to	Lizard	110 days

This year she was sent to the Tyne to discharge and then went on to Mariehamn. At the commencement of her next outward passage, while navigating the narrow waters between Denmark and Sweden, she came to anchor off Copenhagen and, in the process of weighing her anchor, fouled a telegraph cable, severing communications between the two countries at that point. The cost of this escapade to Captain Erikson was in the region of £2,700.

1933	Elsinore	to	Port Victoria	99 days
1934	Port Victoria	to	Queenstown	125 days
	Mariehamn	to	Port Victoria	114 days
1935	Port Germein	to	Falmouth	131 days
	Mariehamn	to	Port Victoria	117 days
1936	Port Germein	to	Falmouth	119 days
	Falmouth	to	Port Victoria	93 days
1937	Port Victoria	to	Falmouth	116 days
	Oslo	to	East London	92 days
	East London	to	Port Lincoln	31 days

From Port Lincoln she moved up the Spencer Gulf to Port Germein to load wheat, sailing for home on July 14th, 1938. This year she bettered the *Archibald Russell*'s time by 2 days when she reached Falmouth 128 days out.

The *Archibald Russell* merited a lengthy mention by the Port Germein schoolchildren in their record, where a newspaper cutting was inserted. The main topic was the re-rigging of the foremast, and there was much speculation as to how it would be done, as there was no crane to assist the crew. The crew demonstrated to an interested group of spectators their independence from the shore by hoisting it with their own gear. A set of brace winches which came from the recently scrapped *Ponape* was fitted to the foremast.

Plate 68 The Penang *loading wheat at Port Germein*
L. Saunders

During her stay, two men deserted the ship. These desertions, which were far from rare, were a constant source of worry to the owner and Captain, as the ship had to pay a £100 fine for each missing sailor. Farmers, eager for cheap labour, would hide and feed them in return for a few weeks' work until the coast was clear. A replacement for one of the missing men was a young Australian called Ron Tilbrook, seventeen years old, who signed the *Archibald Russell*'s articles on April 27th. He was asked to pay £50 for the privilege but only paid £5, not having any more money, and was accepted as not enough young men were coming forward. Times were getting better with the passing of the depression and plenty of jobs ashore. Ron humped his dunnage down the mile-long jetty, accompanied by the Third Mate who painted a hard picture of life aboard. Indeed, he had second thoughts about the venture but his friend Ian McRae from *L'Avenir* also signed on and with his encouragement he decided to go through with it. He soon found the job was no bed of roses, the life under sail being little changed over the years.

The ship was due to leave on May 10th, and on the eve of departure some of the crew went to Port Pirie for a last celebration. Two girls who were still aboard in the small hours were placed in a wheat truck which was then propelled hopefully towards the shore end of the jetty. At first light, the tug was made fast and, although three men had not returned to the ship, the moorings were cast off and the crew made sail, Captain Sjögren not wishing to waste a fair wind by delaying any longer.

The jetty, now completely deserted, would remain so for the next six months. Each time the locals saw the last of the ships sail away, those that depended on them for employment must have wondered how much longer these old windjammers would continue to come. The passing years brought a decline in the fleet in one way or another: collision, stranding, dismasting and the breaker's yard steadily reducing their numbers and on occasion, some unaccountable catastrophe. 1938 was *L'Avenir*'s last appearance. Recently acquired from Captain Erikson by the Hamburg Amerika Line to be used as a training ship, she had been re-named *Admiral Karpfanger* and came to Port Germein after a 107 day passage with 40 cadets among her crew. At the time, the *Archibald Russell* had sailed and there was some doubt about the *Admiral Karpfanger*'s safety as no wireless reports had been received from her for two months. In fact, she sailed into oblivion, no trace every having been found of her, and it was conjectured that she may have collided with an iceberg off Cape Horn. She was the last of the world's sailing fleet to go missing in these wild and lonely latitudes.

Ron Tilbrook soon settled into the *Archibald Russell*'s routine, working aloft and taking his trick at the wheel. He found most of the crew were good shipmates. The sailmaker tried to put the wind up him by telling him that the *Archibald Russell* was a coffin ship, having lost a whole watch overboard while working at the braces. However, no such incident appears in any records and this may have been a variation on the 1928 voyage when two men were lost from the jibboom. As for being a coffin ship, she does not appear to have had any such reputation.

They were 54 days to the Horn. It was midwinter and there was ice about. Also they had their fair share of bad weather. During a particularly heavy squall, the ship took a violent lurch and some of the cargo shifted to leewards. It was at this time that the shortage of crew was most felt. All hands were called out to reduce canvas in a hurry as the lower yards were almost touching the seas, so hard pressed was she. The situation seemed critical and even Captain Sjögren climbed aloft to the mainyard to help make the sail fast. In a situation like this he was worth three men. Later, when everything was more or less under control, those that could be spared went

177

Plate 69 Heaving down the fore-tack
R. Tilbrook

178

Plate 70 Stormy weather off Cape Horn in the Archibald Russell, *1938*
R. Tilbrook

below to trim the cargo and bring the ship back on an even keel.

Off the pitch of the Horn during another gale, she shipped a mighty sea which smashed up two after lifeboats, the starboard one being reduced to matchwood. It also carried away the port poop companionway, two steel water tanks under the break of the poop and the weather mizzen pinrail. Ian McRae was washed clean overboard while the crew stood helpless, unable to assist him, but he managed to grab a rope and hang on for dear life. Unbelievably, he was washed aboard again further aft, where his mates seized him, hauling him to safety. Ron was fortunate in that he saw the sea coming. He was standing by the poop ladder and nipped smartly into the officers' bathroom, banging the door shut behind him.

The Horn had one more go at them before they sailed into more pleasant waters. They were sailing fast at the time, closehauled on the port tack under reduced canvas. She was steering hard with two men at the wheel. Both were sweating in spite of the cold as they tried to keep her on course. A squall struck the ship and the helmsman struggled to put the helm up to run off before the wind, with the Captain and Mate throwing their weight on the spokes to no avail. But the ship was caught aback in a dangerous situation from which they were very fortunate to escape without loss of

179

spars. However, their luck-held and the Horn was passed on July 4th.

It took 76 days to sail the rest of the way, a long passage, perhaps due to the small crew. They did not run short of food but Ron found the quantity and quality left much to be desired from his point of view. He noted that when a pig was killed nothing was wasted: they made pancakes from the blood, much appreciated by the Finns but not by Ron. At one stage he joined in a deputation to the poop complaining that the salt beef was rotten. Captain Sjögren, when asked to taste it, agreed after some blustering that it was uneatable and ordered a fresh meal to be cooked right away.

When they reached the Trades, the heavy sails were sent down, old patched ones taken from the locker and bent in their places. These old sails were a miscellaneous lot, a few coming from ships long since disappeared from the seas, amongst them, Ron noted, some from the *Herzogin Cecilie* and the *Hougomont*. The crew were set to chipping, painting and varnishing until the old ship shone like a new pin. Also a new royal yard was fashioned and sent aloft. As the *Archibald Russell* sailed past the Lizard, she hoisted her flags of recognition and was answered from the signal station with the international code flags S H, followed by A E K P, which told her crew that their discharging port was to be Cork. She was at this time 130 days out and was immediately put about for Queenstown, where she arrived five days later on September 22nd, 1938.

Captain Sjögren left the ship in Cork to take command of the four-masted barque *Moshulu* in Belfast.

Plate 71 Storm damage, 1938
R. Tilbrook

180

Chapter XVIII

Last Voyage

Captain Sommarlund was no stranger to the ship as we know. He rose up from Second to First Mate over the years in the *Archibald Russell*. So now he moved his gear into the Master's quarters and took over command.

Five weeks were occupied in Cork discharging the grain cargo and taking on board 1,150 tons of ballast. It was a time of uncertainty because there was a rumour going around that the ship was to be sold. None the less, Captain Sommarlund received orders to sail to Falmouth for drydocking.

By Saturday, October 29th, all was ready. With a pilot on board the *Archibald Russell* left Cork, but before she reached the open sea, the wind began to freshen from the south-west, bringing with it mist and rain and the promise of stronger winds to come. The anchor was dropped on the advice of the pilot who then left. By midnight, the wind had gone round to the north-west, a favourable quarter. So, at 4 am on Sunday, the Captain decided to sail. However once the anchor was weighed the wind dropped, leaving the *Archibald Russell* drifting towards the sandbanks. A tug was hurriedly signalled but in spite of getting a tow-rope on board she was unable to hold her. Consequently, with the ebb-tide running, the old ship drifted helplessly on to a sandbank where she was forced to remain until next high-water. However, in spite of this initial setback, she came off on the flood and proceeded on her way to Falmouth.

Although the sale of the *Archibald Russell* appeared imminent, Captain Sommarlund's orders were to prepare for a voyage to the Spencer Gulf. By November 5th all was ready. With a crew of 25 and a clean bottom she set off for South Australia, but not before the Captain had received a last message from Captain Erikson that the ship had been sold.

The passage to the Spencer Gulf was made in 89 days, an average passage. Captain Sjögren in his new command, the four-masted barque *Moshulu*, made it in 82 days from Belfast. On arrival at Port Lincoln it turned out that no cargo was immediately available. Good harvests in other parts of the world had reduced the demand for Australian wheat and some of the freights offered were unrealistic. A great gathering of sailing ships lay at anchor off Port Lincoln, hopefully waiting for improved offers. Wild rumours circulated when crews met and exchanged news. Some of the Company's ships were to be sold, it was said. It appears that the Archibald Russell's sale fell through as no further mention of it occurs. Others were to go elsewhere for their home-ward cargoes. In the background of all this were rumours of war.

Eventually the *Archibald Russell* was fixed to load once more at Port Germein. The freight was only 25/- per ton, a great disappointment, and there was going to be precious little profit this voyage. She made her way up the Gulf once again and moored alongside the old jetty with the decrepit-looking and unpopular barque *Winterhude* tied up on the other side. She was at the time short of crew and this was noted by the Port Germein schoolchildren in their journal. Apparently the First Mate had desert-ed and also one seaman. This was a windfall for the *Archibald Russell*'s Second Mate as he was promoted to First Mate. The *Winterhude*'s Third became the *Archibald Russell*'s Second. It was late in the season when she finally cleared Port Germein on April 3rd, 1939.

It was to be her final departure from the Gulf. For years she had come as regularly as the seasons to the lonely anchorage, the friendly harbours, the heat and the flies and might have continued to do so for a few more had not the war, now looming over Europe, brought the trade under sail virtu-ally to an end.

In actual fact she was not the last to leave. The *Killoran* had come late to the Gulf this year. She discharged her wheat in the Tyne, then made her way to the Seychelles for a cargo of guano for New Zealand. After dis-charging the guano at Auckland she sailed for the Spencer Gulf, arriving long after all the other sailers had left. When she finally got away with her wheat it was mid-July and the Second World War had been waging for two months before she reached Queenstown on November 29th, 1939.

Once clear of the Gulf Captain Sommarlund turned the *Archibald Rus-sell* west towards the Cape of Good Hope. The ensuing passage was leisurely, occupying 121 days before making Falmouth on August 2nd, 1939. Her last homecoming was as peaceful and beautiful as anyone could wish on this warm summer's day, with the holidaymakers swarming the beaches. One of them, Richard Young, hired a boat and went out to meet her. She sailed in with a gentle breeze, clewing up her lighter sails as she approached the anchorage. Then, with her mizzen yards aback and the headway checked, the anchor was let go. He photographed her as she was in the process of doing this.

Orders were received to proceed to Hull and away she went with every sail drawing, an unforgettable sight to those fortunate to see her set sail that day. After a leisurely passage up channel, she was taken in tow by the tug *Englishman* of the United Towing Co. Ltd., 13 miles north of the East Goodwin Light Vessel, the price for this service being £120. When she got

Plate 72 Coming to anchor, Falmouth Bay, August 2nd 1939.
R. Young

there she was docked in the Alexandra Basin, where she lay discharging her cargo into keels and barges which transported it to the mills. Before she had completed, war broke out and as a result she never again left the shores of England. Several of her consorts continued sailing, meeting various fates due to the fortunes of war, but the *Archibald Russell* was the only one to lie idle and out of commission, away from her home port of Mariehamn.

Why was she permitted to rust away in port while she might have been profitably employed elsewhere? The danger and uncertainty of sending her to sea were factors. Erikson's four-masted barque *Olivebank* had already fallen victim to a mine off the coast of Denmark with the loss of her Captain and thirteen of her complement. The *Archibald Russell*'s crew which brought her home from Australia were soon dispersed: Captain Sommarlund signed on a steamship and sailed as First Mate of her; others drifted away one by one until only the Second Mate and a Hungarian seaman remained. Under these circumstances, she was laid up in the safety of the Humber until the situation improved sufficiently to send her to sea again. Since it appeared likely to be a long time Arthur Söderlund, one of Erikson's Captains, came aboard with a party to send down some of the

183

Plate 73   Entering Hull, 1939
Photo by permission of Hull Daily Mail

upper yards and generally prepare her for lay-up.

Autumn turned to winter and with Finland engaged in a life-and-death struggle with Russia, it was not until March, 1940, that preparations were made to put the *Archibald Russell* into commission. At the time, there was talk of a grain charter from the Argentine to Britain. Accordingly a crew was assembled in Åland with orders to make their way to Hull to prepare her for the voyage. Captain Uno Mörn was appointed Master and duly set off with seven men to go by train across Sweden and Norway to Bergen, where they were to take the steamer to England. It was a race against time. Soon after they set off the Germans invaded Norway. In fact Captain Mörn and his men arrived too late. The Germans were at the gates of Bergen and the last steamer had sailed.

Another party in charge of the First Mate, Borge Borenius, also set off for Hull. Their journey was likewise disrupted by the invasion. After reaching Bergen and finding no steamer for England, Borenius shepherded his crew 150 miles up the coast to Ålesund. Here they were fortunate to get aboard the last ship for England which however, because of all the Naval activity, was diverted to Scapa Flow. Eventually they reached Hull, but not so Captain Mörn's party. They got no further than Bergen and were forced to return home, travelling much of the way on foot.

The failure to assemble a complete crew sealed the *Archibald Russell*'s fate. She was trapped in Hull indefinitely while the bombs rained down and the Spitfires wheeled overhead in defence of their country.

The *Killoran* was now the only one of John Hardie & Co.'s old ships still actually engaged in trade. It will be remembered that she was late leaving the Spencer Gulf after taking a cargo of guano to Auckland. She sailed from Port Lincoln on July 13th, and was 130 days to Queenstown. She discharged her cargo at Cork and was towed across to the Bristol Channel in the New Year of 1940, to load a coal cargo for the Argentine. She sailed from Cardiff in February, making a leisurely passage of 65 days to Buenos Aires where, after discharging her coal, she loaded 2,500 tons of maize and 500 tons of sugar and sailed on June 15th. Her destination was Las Palmas in the Canary Islands, though whether this was her port of discharge or merely a port of call for orders is not clear, but she never made it. She was 56 days out and still some 500 miles from her destination when a German raider put a shot across her bow, at which the Master, Captain Leman, ordered the mainyard aback and waited for the boarding party. War being what it was, there was no sympathy from the German commander for the old sailing ship and he gave orders for her to be sunk. The date was August 10th, 1940.

It was some time before the news of her loss filtered through. She was

Plate 74 The Killoran
W. Ball

posted officially as missing in early November, 1940. On December 7th
the general public was able to read an article by the shipping historian
Frank C. Bowen in the *Journal of Commerce* of the loss of the *Killoran*
and also the death of her previous owner, Mr. James Hardie, who had
passed away in Glasgow. He was seventy-three years old and until his
death still maintained his office at 11, Bothwell Street. The business was
wound up soon after and as Frank Bowen pointed out in his article, it was
a curious and melancholy fact that the two announcements had come on
the same day, marking the end of a particular era.

In June, 1941, the German invasion of Russia threw Finland on the side
of the Axis, making her technically at war with Great Britain. The
Archibald Russell, with other Finnish ships, was seized by the Admiralty
Marshal as a prize of war. This did not change her fortunes in any way. It
was never contemplated by the British authorities to send her to sea again.
Various departments were always crying out for ships for some service or

other—storage, bargework or accommodation—and eventually she became a storeship for the Ministry of Food.

The chance of her going to sea again under sail was considerably lessened when it was decided to reduce the height of her tophamper. She was rigged down to her lower masts and all the spars sent ashore. Ron Tilbrook, at the time serving with the RAF as an air-gunner, saw her several times when he was stationed at Elsham Wolds. She was a sorry sight which saddened him, knowing her as she used to be. She was taken to Goole and spent the rest of the war there.

During this time of neglect and misuse, she came under the charge of Captain David Williams, a man who appreciated her true worth as a sailing ship. This wiry little Welshman, at sixty-eight, should have been enjoying a peaceful retirement after a lifetime at sea, but preferred to make himself useful in some capacity, however humble, providing it contributed to the war effort. The command of the hulk does not sound a very inspiring job, but he made the most of it and in fact had quite an affection for her, having known her in the past.

Captain Williams' career was quite a remarkable one, much of it having been spent in sail. He served many years with the White Star Line and at one time had been Chief Officer in their sail-training ship *Mersey*. During the 1914-1918 War he commanded Devitt & Moore's training ship, the four-masted barque *Medway*, in which he accomplished some smart passages including one record of 42 days from Tocopilla to Cape Town which stands to this day. In 1922, he sailed the huge four-masted barque *Bellands* to Australia and back, making good passages both ways.[1]

A *Daily Mail* reporter interviewed him on board the *Archibald Russell* in 1945 and, according to him, the Captain waxed quite poetic about her. He even allowed himself a little flight of fancy, saying that he hoped that one day she would be re-rigged and sent once more to sea as a training ship, if possible with him in command. There were others who had this same dream, but it was never to be.

The end of the hostilities brought no immediate reprieve from her humble occupation. During 1946, there was some move to return her to her owners. It was decided that she should be towed to the Tyneside shipyard of Swan, Hunter & Wigham Richardson Ltd. at Wallsend. The spars were loaded on deck and it looked hopeful that she might be restored, although anyone who knew her in her prime and paid her a visit at this time would not have rated her chances very high. She was in a terrible state, with her jibboom shorn of rigging; all the yards, together with the topgallants and topmasts, were piled on deck and rusty blocks littered around. One person who did not share this view was Captain Erikson, who was trying his best to get his sailing ships back in business again.

In October, 1946, Captain Sommarlund was sent to take command of his old ship. In Goole he engaged an officer and eight riggers to help with the tow to Newcastle. This short voyage was not altogether without incident as Mr Harvey Lyne, the Merchant Navy Officer in charge of the riggers, related. Before they left the Humber a gale warning was received and Captain Sommarlund decided to bring up for the night. Accordingly, the anchor was let go and riding lights hoisted. The riggers made themselves comfortable in the fo'c'sle with the large iron stove well stoked up, while the Captain and Mate retired to the comfort of the after accommodation where Captain Erikson's portrait still decorated the saloon. Mr Lyne, while keeping anchor watch, heard the fo'c'sle door open and the sound of footsteps approaching. He expected one of the riggers coming to report to him, but no-one appeared. It was eerie, but not being a superstitious man he took little notice. When the click of the door lock occurred again, followed by the ghostly footsteps, he decided to investigate. He thought the door might have a defective lock, swinging open with the slight rolling of the ship. However, on examination he could find nothing wrong with it, neither could he account for the footsteps although they sounded real enough to record the episode in a letter to Ron Tilbrook a few years later.

Next morning steam was raised on the donkey boiler. The belt drive from the winch to the windlass was rigged, but this kept parting and in the end all hands had to man the capstan, tramping round and round until the anchor came home. The passage to Wallsend took about 30 hours.

In March, 1947, she was officially released by the Ministry of Transport on temporary charter to Captain Erikson and work was started on her. It was bound to be a long job to repair the ravages of eight years of neglect, and not much progress had been made when he suddenly died in August, 1947. This threw the future of his sailing ships in doubt and work on the *Archibald Russell* was suspended. She was taken to Dunston-on-Tyne, where she was moored to buoys and put on the market for sale for £5,000.

There were enquiries but no takers. There was talk of an Italian gentleman buying her to put in the River Plate trade, but nothing came of it. She nearly became a floating restaurant but that also fell through. There were appeals from people who wanted her preserved as a monument but nothing was done, and finally she was purchased by the British Iron and Steel Corporation. She was moved to the yard of J.J. King & Co. at Gateshead-on-Tyne for breaking up. It was during this period that Richard Keys, a fourteen-year-old youth with a passion for old sailing ships, snapped her with his Brownie box camera. She was lying at Tyne Main at the time, and he captured what were among the last pictures taken of her before the oxy-acetylene torches were put to her.

That is almost the finish of the story. Had her end been delayed a few more years she most certainly would have finished up as a museum piece, a fine example of a Scottish four-master. Fifteen years later the remoter harbours of the world were being scoured for such specimens. However, it was not to be, but the memory will linger for many years on account of the numerous models of her which exist. Harold Underhill, an authority on sailing ships, produced authentic plans for model makers, the details of which were taken from the original plans obtained from Captain Erikson just before the Second World War. More recently Edward Bowness, A.I.N.A., who knew her well in her sailing days, produced a book called *The Four-Masted Barque*. The fact that the *Archibald Russell* was the main feature in the book ensured a further spate of models. The bell and the wheel found their way into a public house.

With her disappearance, the firm of J. Hardie & Co. and their sailing ships became just a memory.

As for the *Archibald Russell*, people on the whole regarded her with affection, the romantic ship with an unromantic name.

Plate 75 End of the road. The Archibald Russell
at Tyne Main, August 1947
Richard E. Keys

189

Fleet List

Name	Rig	Official Number	Tonnages	Dimensions	Remarks	
Inch Moan	Iron barque	73851	817 gross 780 net	196.2 x 32.0 x 18.7 ft	4.7.1876	Launched by D. & W. Henderson & Co., Glasgow (Yard No. 171) for Clutha Shipping Co.
					14.4.77	Wrecked at Old Port of San Antonia, Chile, whilst on passage Valparaiso-Liverpool, copper, wheat, sugar.
Inch Marnock	Iron barque	73864	824 gross 787 net	197.1 x 32.0 x 18.4 ft	21.9.1876	Launched by D. & W. Henderson & Co., Glasgow (Yard No. 172) for Clutha Shipping Co. J. Hardie.
					1885 25.1.1887	Foundered off Algoa Bay, 30.05S, 35.58E (Indian Ocean whilst on passage Java-Channel for orders, sugar.
Inch Kenneth	Iron ship	76728	1120 gross 1074 net	217.1 x 34.5 x 20.7 ft	16.11.1876	Launched by D. & W. Henderson & Co., Glasgow (Yard No. 173) for Clutha Shipping Co.
					4.9.1877	Foundered 34.50S, 24.30 S (Indian Ocean) while on passage Calcutta- Hull ... wheat and linseed ... 18 lost out of 26 crew.

Name	Rig	Official Number	Tonnages	Dimensions	Remarks	
Inch Keith	Iron ship	78597	1298 gross 1238 net	236.3 x 35.5 x 21.5 ft	3.4.1878	Launched by Barclay, Curle & Co., Glasgow (Yard No. 283) as a full-rigged ship for Clutha Shipping Co.
					1880	Re-rigged as a barque.
					1886	Owner became John Hardie
					1889	Owner became J. Hardie & Co.
					1897	Sold to Massone & Repetto, Italy and renamed *Fede.*
					1908	Sold to G. Celle Uva Repetto, Italy.
					1915	Sold to A. Di Plaisant, Italy.
					29.8.1916	Torpedoed and sunk in the Mediterranean
Inch Murren	Iron ship	78635	1318 gross 1254 net	231.1 x 35.8 x 21.5 ft	2.7.1878	Launched by Birrell, Stenhouse & Co., Dumbarton (Yard No. 30) for Clutha Shipping Co.
					1886	Owner became John Hardie.
					24.11.1888	Abandoned on fire (spontaneous combustion) 14.41S, 35.13W S. Atlantic while on passage Iquique-Falmouth, nitrate of soda.
Salamanca	Iron ship	76758	1262 gross 1202 net	227.7 x 35.8 x 21.3 ft	1886	Taken over by John Hardie.
					1897	Sold to Semidei Brothers, Italy.
					1903	Owners became Fratelli A. & G. Semideii.
					1914	Broken up at Genoa.

Name	Rig	Official Number	Tonnages	Dimensions	Remarks	
Orthes	Iron ship	78563	1270 gross 1206 net	228.0 x 35.8 21.4 ft	9.11.1877	Launched by James & George Thomson, Clydebank, Glasgow (Yard No. 157) as *Orthes* for A. Russell and others, Glasgow.
					1885	Taken over by J. Hardie.
					1889	Owners J. Hardie & Co.
					1897	Sold to M. Bruusgaard, Norway and renamed *Mataura*.
					1898	Owners Akties 'Mataura' (M. Bruusgaard).
					1904	Management transferred to K. Bruusgaard.
					1915	Sold to A/S Hedvig (M. Hannestad manager) Norway and renamed *Hedvig*.
					9.5.1917	Abandoned in the North Atlantic whilst on a voyage from Newport News via Halifax to Christiania with a cargo of coal.
Talavera	Iron 4 masted barque	86668	1796 gross 1730 net	266.2 x 40.0 x 23.6 ft	19.6.1882	Launched by Birrell, Stenhouse & Co., Dumbarton (Yard No. 35) for John Hardie.
					1889	John Hardie & Co.
					1.5.1896	Wrecked on Santa Maria Island while on passage Valparaiso-Concepcion Bay, ballast.

Name	Rig	Official Number	Tonnages	Dimensions	Remarks
Albuera	Steel full-rigged ship	90058	1554 gross 1502 net	236.6 x 39.2 x 22.8 ft	19.5.1885 Launched by James & George Thomson, Clydebank, Glasgow (Yard No. 225) for John Hardie.
					John Hardie & Co.
					1889
					1900 Reduced to barque.
					1911 Sold to T. Brovig, Farsund. Renamed *Cis*.
					1916 Sold to Skibsakties Fremad (J.M. Jacobsen & Co., managers), Norway and renamed *Fremad 1*.
					9.4.1917 Torpedoed and sunk in the North Sea.

Name	Rig	Official Number	Tonnages	Dimensions	Remarks
Aberlemno	Iron barque	73832	771 gross 750 net	184.4 x 31.0 x 18.5 ft	25.5.1876 Launched by Birrell, Stenhouse & Co., Dumbarton (Yard No. 14) as *Aberlemno* for David T. Boyd, Glasgow.
					1880 Sold to Aber Shipping Co., Glasgow.
					1882 Transferred to North British Shipping Co., Glasgow.
					1884 H. Grierson & G. Cowper managers of above.
					1885 Transferred to J. Hardie & Co.
					1889 Sold to M. Tutton, Swansea.
					1905 Sold to Skibakties Durban (A.J. Grefstad manager), Norway, and renamed *Durban*.
					1912 Sold to Skibakties Halewood (same manager) Norway.
					1914 Sold to Akties Durban (J. Jacobsen manager), Norway.
					1917 Management transferred to Andr. Hannestad.
					1918 Sold to Akties Sando (Christianssand Shipping Co. Ltd. manager), Norway. Fitted with a 4-cylinder oil engine by Lysekils M.V., A/B Lysekil.
					1919 Sold to Christianssands Motoreil A/S (same manager), Norway.
					1920 Sold to W. Millar, Sweden and renamed *Mary*.
					1923 Broken up at Hamburg.

Name	Rig	Official Number	Tonnages	Dimensions	Remarks
Dallam Tower	Iron ship	54541	1499 gross 1499 net	243.7 x 38.3 x 23.9 ft	12.8.1866 Launched by G.R. Clover & Co., Birkenhead (Yard No. 12) as *Dallam Tower* for Lancaster Shipowners Co. Ltd. of Liverpool. 1882 Sold to D. Duncan of Rothesay. 1885 Sold to J. Forrester of Glasgow, J. Hardie & Co. managers. 23.2.1889 Stranded while on passage Newcastle, N.S.W. to Probolingo off Tanjong Slokke, Java and abandoned.
Brambletye	Iron ship	73627	1544 gross 1495 net	241.8 x 39.2 x 23.1 ft	28.1.1876 Launched by Barrow Shipbuilding Co. Ltd., Barrow (Yard No. 26) for W.R. Price & Co., London. 1887 Sold to W. & J. Crawford, Glasgow. 1890 Sold to J. Hay, Glasgow. 1891 Taken over by J. Hardie & Co. 1909 Sold to Naam. Venn Scheepswerf De Kooptrandel and broken up in Holland.
Vimeira	Steel 4-masted barque	98650	2233 gross 2163 net	283.4 x 42.5 x 24.7 ft	19.6.1891 Launched by C. Connell & Co. 7.1891 Completed. 1924 Sold to T.G. Duriaz and broken up in France.

Name	Rig	Official Number	Tonnages	Dimensions	Remarks	
Pyrenees	Steel 4-masted barque	98670	2243 gross 2169 net	284.5 x 42.5 x 24.7 ft	7.9.1891	Launched by C. Connell & Co., Glasgow (Yard No. 178) for John Hardie & Co.
					9.1891	Completed.
					16.11.1900	Caught fire on passage Tacoma to Leith.
					2.12.1900	Reached Sanatul Is., Mangareva Group. Abandoned.
					1902	Refloated. Sold to I.E. Thayer, U.S.A.
					1905	Sold to Ship Manga Reva Co. (I.E. Thayer, manager) U.S.A. and renamed *Manga Reva*.
					1916	Sold to Brynhilda Shipping Corporation, U.S.A.
					2.11.1916	Sailed from Rotterdam to Hampton Roads in ballast.
					19.11.1916	Reported in 47N 14W and subsequently disappeared.
Saragossa	Steel 4-masted barque	115737	2503 gross 2262 net	289.9 x 43.3 x 24.5 ft	4.9.1902	(Yard No. 137) by the Dundee Shipbuilders' Co. Ltd., Dundee.
					15.8.1904	Wrecked at Mangaia, Cook Islands, whilst on a voyage from Newcastle, N.S.W. to San Francisco with a cargo of coal.

Name	Rig	Official Number	Tonnages	Dimensions	Remarks	
Hougomont	Steel 4-masted barque	105093	2428 gross 2261 net	292.4 x 43.2 x 24.1 ft	3.6.1897	Launched by Scott & Co., Greenock (Yard No. 346) for Hougomont Sailing Ship Co. Ltd. (John Hardie & Co., managers).
					1897	Completed
					1902	Owners became J. Hardie & Co.
					1925	Sold to Gustaf Erikson, Finland.
Nivelle	Steel 4-masted barque	106074	2430 gross 2262 net	292.4 x 43.2 x 24.2 ft	20.5.1897	Launched by Scott & Co., Greenock (Yard No. 345) for Nivelle Sailing Ship Co. Ltd. (J. Hardie & Co. managers). Completed.
					1900	Owners became J. Hardie & Co.
					20.6.1906	Wrecked at Point Grande, off Antofagasta on a voyage from Newcastle, N.S.W. to Antofagasta with a cargo of coal.
Corunna	Steel 4-masted barque	102633	2432 gross 2268 net	293.0 x 43.0 x 24.4 ft	30.8.1893	Launched by D. & W. Henderson & Co., Glasgow (Yard No. 369) for Corunna Sailing ship Co. Ltd., (John Hardie & Co. managers).
					10.1893	Completed.
					30.8.1904	Stranded at Miramar. Refloated and brought to Montevideo.
					1905	Hulked in Montevideo.
					1917	Re-rigged and renamed *La Epoca*.
					1922	Out of register.

Name	Rig	Official Number	Tonnages	Dimensions	Remarks	
Archibald Russell	Steel 4-masted barque	121209	2385 gross 2181 net	291.4 x 43.2 x 24.1 ft	23.1.1905	Launched by Scotts' Shipbuilding & Engineering Co. Ltd. (Yard No. 391) for James, John, Jackson and William Russell. Managers J. Hardie & Co.
					3.1.1924	Sold to Captain Gustaf Erikson, Mariehamn.
					1941	Taken over by the Ministry of Food as a storeship based at Goole.
					1946	Towed to Tyneside to the yard of Swan Hunter & Wigham Richardson Ltd. for repairs.
					23.4.47	Released by Ministry of Food and returned to Captain Erikson's ownership. On his death in the same year she was put up for sale.
					1949	Broken up by J.J. King & Co. at Gateshead-on-Tyne.

Name	Rig	Official Number	Tonnages	Dimensions	Remarks
Kildalton	Steel barque	115739	1784 gross 1591 net	261.4 x 39.2 x 22.7 ft	29.11.1902 Launched by Ailsa Shipbuilding Co. Ltd., Troon (Yard No. 109) as *Kildalton* for Kildalton Barque Co. Ltd. (J. Browne, manager), Glasgow. 2.1903 Completed. 1909 J. Hardie & Co. became managers of Kildalton Barque Co. Ltd. 12.12.1914 Captured by the German commerce raider *Prinz Eitel Friedrich* when 870 miles SW 3/4 S (true) from Valparaiso whilst on a voyage from Liverpool to Callao with general cargo, and sunk by bombs. Crew taken on board the raider and 31.12.14 landed at Easter Island until 26.2.1915 when rescued by a Swedish vessel and taken to Panama ... arrived there 12.3.1915.
Killoran	Steel barque	111283	1757 gross 1569 net	261.5 x 39.1 x 22.7 ft	30.6.1900 Launched by Ailsa Shipbuilding Co., Troon (Yard No. 88) for Killoran Barque Co. Ltd. (J. Browne, manager), Glasgow. 8.1900 Completed. 1909 J. Hardie & Co. became managers. 1924 Sold to Gustaf Erikson, Finland.

Name	Rig	Official Number	Tonnages	Dimensions	Remarks	
Kilmeny	Steel barque	104559	1630 gross 1469 net	256.5 x 38.2 x 21.4 ft	21.6.1894	Launched by Ailsa Shipbuilding Co., Troon (Yard No. 45) as *Kilmeny* for Kilmeny Barque Co. Ltd. (J. Browne, manager), Glasgow.
					10.1894	Completed.
					1909	J. Hardie & Co. become managers.
					1923	Sold to J. Tuul and broken up in Germany.
Almora	Steel barque	102374	1856 gross 1769 net	257.8 x 39.2 x 22.9 ft	6.6.1893	Launched by Wm. Hamilton & Co., Port Glasgow (Yard No. 108) as *Almora* for Almora Ship Co Ltd (W. & J. Crawford, managers), Greenock.
					7.1893	Completed.
					1898	Managers become D. Corsar & Sons, Liverpool.
					1909	J. Hardie & Co. appointed managers.
					1911	Sold to Akties Almora (M.H. Gundersen manager), Norway.
					1913	Purchased by Akties Almora (S.W. Marcussen, manager), Norway.
					1916	A.H. Torbjornsen became manager.
					2.1921	Dismasted ... reached port ... no further details.

Name	Rig	Official Number	Tonnages	Dimensions	Remarks
Monkbarns	Steel ship	105321	1911 gross 1771 net	267.0 x 40.1 x 23.6 ft	20.6.1895 Launched by A. McMillan & Son. Ltd., Dumbarton (Yard No. 333) as *Monkbarns* for Charles W. Corsar, Liverpool. 7.1895 Completed. 1901 Owners became D. Corsar & Sons, Liverpool. J. Hardie & Co. appointed managers 1909 Sold to John Stewart & Co., Liverpool. 1911 1927 Sold to Spanish owners and reduced to a hulk
Fairport	Steel ship	105381	1996 gross 1857 net	265.9 x 40.0 x 23.5 ft	27.3.1896 Launched by Russell & Co., Port Glasgow (Yard No. 386) for Charles W. Corsar, Liverpool. 4.1896 Completed. 1901 Owners became D. Corsar & Sons, Liverpool. J. Hardie & Co. appointed manaagers. 1909 Sold to R. Salvesen & Co., Norway. 1910 Sold to Akties Christianssand (S.O. Stray & Co. managers), Norway and renamed *Spangereid*. 1915 2.10.1920 Burnt out at St. Helena whilst on a voyage from Delagoa Bay to Gothenburg with a cargo of coal.

Name	Rig	Official Number	Tonnages	Dimensions	Remarks
Musselcrag	Steel barque	106792	1985 gross 1871 net	266.6 x 40.0 x 23.7 ft	26.5.1896 Launched by Wm. Hamilton & Co., Port Glasgow (Yard No. 126) as *Musselcrag* for Charles W. Corsar, Liverpool.
					6.1896 Completed
					1901 Owners became D. Corsar & Sons, Liverpool.
					1909 J. Hardie & Co. appointed managers.
					1910 Sold to Akties Musselcrag (A. Bech & Co. managers), Norway.
					1916 Sold to Thv. B. Heistein & Sons, Norway and renamed *Astrella*.
					16.11.1916 Abandoned at sea whilst on a voyage in ballast from Leith to Montevideo (for orders).
Pegasus	Iron 4-masted ship	91147	2631 gross 2564 net	314.0 x 42.3 x 24.9 ft	24.7.1884 Launched by W.H. Potter & Sons, Liverpool (Yard No. 119) as *Pegasus* for W.T. Dixon & Sons, Liverpool.
					1892 Sold to Charles W. Corsar, Liverpool.
					1897 Reduced to barque.
					1901 Owners became D. Corsar & Sons, Liverpool.
					1909 J. Hardie & Co. appointed managers.
					1910 Sold to Akties Pegasus (Chr, Nielsen & Co. managers), Norway.
					10.9.1912 Stranded at Mariehamn whilst on a voyage from Sundsvall to Melbourne with a cargo of planed boards. Refloated and taken in tow for Stockholm, beached at Furusund, became total loss.

Name	Rig	Official Number	Tonnages	Dimensions	Remarks	
Chiltonford	Steel 4-masted barque	99866	2348 gross 2198 net	298.8 x 44.0 x 24.5 ft	19.11.1892	Launched by Fairfield Shipbuilding & Engineering Co. Ltd., Glasgow (Yard No. 368) for Chiltonford Ship Co. Ltd. (Briggs, Harvie & Co., managers), Glasgow.
					12.1892	Completed.
					1898	D. Corsar & Sons, Liverpool become managers.
					1899	C.W. Corsar manager.
					1901	Management from C.W. Corsar to D. Corsar & Sons.
					1910	J. Hardie & Co. appointed managers.
					1912	Sold to G. Windram & Co., Liverpool.
					1915	Sold To Akties Olivebank (E. Monsen & Co., managers) Norway and renamed *Chile*.
					1916	Sold A/S Oddero (Thv. B. Heistein & Sons A/S managers), Norway and renamed *Asalia*.
					30.8.1917	Torpedoed and sunk off S.W. Ireland.

Name	Rig	Official Number	Tonnages	Dimensions	Remarks	
Clevedon	Iron ship	69328	1835 gross 1778 net	261.6 x 41.8 x 23.8 ft	22.11.1873	Launched by Potter & Hodginson, Liverpool (Yard No. 46) as Chrysomene for H. Fernie & Sons, Liverpool.
					1890	Owners became Liverpool Shipping Co. Ltd., (H. Fernie & Sons, managers).
					1901	Sold to E.C. Schramm & Co., Germany and renamed Elfrieda.
					1909	Sold to Aug. Bolen, Wm. Miller, S. Nachf., Germany.
					1914	Sold to Vinnen Gebruder, Germany.
					4.8.1914	Seized whilst lying at Bristol after arriving from Sydney, condemned as a prize. Requisitioned by the Admiralty. Renamed Clevedon, registered in London. J. Hardie & Co. appointed managers.
					1921	Sold to Scott Fell & Co., Sydney, N.S.W. and reduced to a coal hulk.
					1923	Sold to Fremantle Coal Co. Ltd. and employed as hulk.
					1930	Taken out to sea and scuttled.

204

Name	Rig	Official Number	Tonnages	Dimensions	Remarks
John Hardie	Steel steamship	121311	4372 gross 2816 net	375.4 x 52.2 x 25.5 ft	1.3.1906 Launched by Wm. Hamilton & Co. Ltd., Port Glasgow (Yard No. 184) for Clutha Shipping Co. Ltd. Three-cylinder triple expansion steam engines made by J.C. Kincaid & Co., Greenock.
					6.9.1915 Captured by the German submarine *U.33* when 98 miles from Cape Finisterre whilst on a voyage from Java to Glasgow with a cargo of sugar and sunk by gunfire. One member of her crew was lost.
Caldergrove	Steel steamship	128276	4327 gross 2809 net	376.8 x 52.3 x 25.5 ft	19.4.1909 Launched by Wm. Hamilton & Co. Ltd., Port Glasgow (Yard No. 204) for Clutha Shipping Co. Ltd. Three-cylinder triple expansion steam engine made by D. Rowan & Co., Glasgow.
					2.6.1909 Completed.
					6.3.1917 Torpedoed and sunk by a German submarine when 200 miles W.N.W. from the Fastnet. The Master and 18 other members of her crew were lost.

References

Chapter 1

1 p1   *Glasgow Herald*, 24 January 1905.
2 p1   Bowen, Frank C. 1935. *Sailing Ships of the London River*.
        London: Sampson Low & Co Ltd., p75.
3 p2   *Colliery Guardian*, 22 April 1904.
4 p3   Original Apprentice's Indenture signed by John Hardie.
        Strathclyde Archives.
5 p3   Letters in possession of Mrs Ethel Hardie.
6 p3   Bowen, Frank C. 1940. Article in *Journal of Commerce*, 7 December.
7 p4   Letters in possession of Mrs Ethel Hardie.
8 p5   Minutes of the Clutha Shipping Company.

Chapter II

1 p7   Lubbock, Basil. 1925. *The Log of the* Cutty Sark.
        Glasgow: James Brown & Son, p235.
2 p8   Lubbock, Basil. 1948. *The Last of the Windjammers*.
        Glasgow: Brown, Son & Ferguson Ltd., Vol I, p317.
3 p11 Minutes of the Clutha Shipping Company.
4 p16 Lubbock, Basil. 1925. *The Log of the* Cutty Sark.
        Glasgow: James Brown & Son, p302.
5 p18 Lubbock, Basil. 1948. *The Last of the Windjammers*.
        Glasgow: Brown, Son & Ferguson Ltd., Vol I, p23-28.
6 p21 *Lloyds' Register of Shipping*.
7 p22 Mitchell Library.

Chapter III

1 p25 Lubbock, Basil. 1925. *The Log of the* Cutty Sark.
        Glasgow: James Brown & Son, p368.
2 p25 Lubbock, Basil. 1948. *The Last of the Windjammers*.
        Glasgow: Brown, Son & Ferguson Ltd., Vol II, p231.
3 p28 Lubbock, Basil. 1948. *The Last of the Windjammers*.
        Glasgow: Brown, Son & Ferguson Ltd., Vol I, p32.

Chapter IV

1 p29 Correspondence between Scotts' Shipbuilding & Engineering
        Co and J. Hardie & Co.
2 p32 Letter from Mr A. Mylne, 15 January 1904.
3 p35 *The Seagoer Magazine*, Spring 1951.

Chapter VI

1 p50 Lloyds' Masters' Records held in the Guildhall Library, Aldermanbury.
2 p50 Bowen, Frank C. 1935. *Sailing Ships of the London River*.
        London: Sampson Low & Co Ltd., p153.
3 p53 Articles of Agreement.
4 p54 Learmont, Captain J. 1950. *Master in Sail*.
        London: Percival Marshall & Co Ltd, p95.
5 p54 Lubbock, Basil. 1932. *The Nitrate Clippers*.
        Glasgow: Brown Son & Ferguson Ltd.
6 p55 Letter from Mr J. Rogers to Mr R. Tilbrook
7 p55 Official Logbook. The account of the *Archibald Russell*'s
        troubles came from this source.

Chapter VII

1 p67 Hatch, Captain N.G., Master of the *Avoca*. November1924.
        Account in *Sea Breezes*.
2 p69 Dickson, Captain H.M. 1933. *Million Miles in Sail*.
        London: Hurst & Blackett Ltd.

Chapter VIII

1 p70 Lloyds' Masters' Records held in the Guildhall Library, Aldermanbury.
2 p73 Angiers, E.A.V. *Fifty Years of Freight*.
        Other freight rates are drawn from this source
3 p75 Lloyds' Masters' Records held in the Guildhall Library,
        Aldermanbury.
4 p76 Lubbock, Basil. 1948. *The Last of the Windjammers*.
        Glasgow: Brown, Son & Ferguson Ltd., Vol II, p278.
5 p79 Robinson, Nancy.1976. *The Reluctant Harbour: The Romance of Port
        Pirie*. Jamestown, South Australia: Nadjuri Australia.

Chapter IX

1 p81 Lloyds' Masters' Records held in the Guildhall Library, Aldermanbury.
2 p81 Bowen, Frank C. 1935. *Sailing Ships of the London River*.
        London: Sampson Low & Co. Ltd., p77.
2 p87 HMSO. August 1919. *Navy Losses and Merchant Shipping
        (Losses)*. From a reprint by Patrick Stevens Ltd, 1979.

Chapter X

1   p90   HMSO. August 1919. *Navy Losses and Merchant Shipping (Losses)*. From a reprint by Patrick Stevens Ltd, 1979. All losses in this chapter come from this source.
2   p95   United States Customs Archives.
3   p99   Official Logbook entry by Captain Buchan.
4   p99   Lubbock, Basil. 1925. *The Log of the* Cutty Sark Glasgow: James Brown & Son, p381.
5   p101   Lindsey, Captain Murray (ex-apprentice of the Killoran).n.d. Account of the *Killoran*'s wartime activities.

Chapter XI

1   p104   Angier, E.A.V.*Fifty Years of Freight*.
2   p104   Bowen, Frank C. 1935. *Sailing Ships of the London River*. London: Sampson Low & Co Ltd., p154.
3   p110   Course, Captain A.G. 1950 *The Wheel's Kick and the Wind's Song*. London: Percival Marshall, p190.

Chapter XII

1   p113   Annual Report of the Chamber of Shipping.
2   p116   Course, Captain A.G. 1950. *The Wheel's Kick and the Wind's Song*. London: Percival Marshall, p187.
3   p125   Kåhre, G. 1978. *The Last Tall Ships*. Greenwich: Conway Maritime Press. The prices J. Hardie received for the *Archibald Russell*, the *Killoran* and the *Hougomont* appear in Chapter V.

Chapter XIII

1   p127   Kåhre, G. 1978. *The Last Tall Ships*. Greenwich: Conway Maritime Press, p121.

Chapter XIV

1   p137   Kåhre, G. 1978. *The Last Tall Ships*. Greenwich: Conway Maritime Press, p31.
2   p139   *Sea Breezes*, February 1960, p85. 'Captain Alexander Backman of Mariehamn'.
3   p139   Lubbock, Basil. 1948. *The Last of the Windjammers*. Glasgow: Brown, Son & Ferguson Ltd., Vol II, p309.
4   p140   Kåhre, G. 1978. *The Last Tall Ships*. Greenwich: Conway Maritime Press, p154.

Chapter XV

1. p144 Butlin, Commander C.M. 1935. *White Sails Crowding*.
London: Jonathan Cape, p35.
2 p146 Attiwell, K. 1930. *Horizon*. London: Jonathan Cape, p103.
3 p150 Correspondence from Harry E. Meadows of Port Augusta,
South Australia.
4 p150 *Western Daily Press*, August 1929.
5 p151 Desmond, Shaw. 1932. *Windjammer*. London: Hutchison & Co. Ltd, p182.

Chapter XVI

1 p152 Letters from Captain Raoul Rasmassen.
2 p157 This account of the *Hougomont*'s dismasting comes from Captain
Alexander Backman's article in *Sea Breezes*, February 1960.
3 p162 Villiers, A.J. 1932. Letter to *Sea Breezes*, September.
4 p165 *Adelaide Advertiser*, January 8th 1933.

Chapter XVII

1 p169 Letter from Nancy Robinson, South Australia.
2 p173 Letters from Claude Beneke.
3 p174 Letters from Claude Beneke.

Chapter XVIII

1 p187 Course, Captain A.J. 1961. *Painted Ports*. London: Hollis & Carter, p189.

General Index

Adams, Capt. J., 4
Åland, 137, 173, 185
Anderson, Eben, 120
Archibald Russel Ltd., 104
Arnot, James, 4
Atkins, Capt. Thomas, 80
Auld, Capt., 112, 114, 116-118

Backman, Capt. Alexander, 157, 159
Beneke, Claude, 171, 172, 174
Birrell, Stenhouse & Co., 14, 19
Borenius, Borge, 185
Bowen, Frank C., 186
Bowness, A.I.N.A. Edward, 189
British Iron & Steel Corporation, 188
Blair, Capt., 3
Brown, James, 52
Browne & Co., J., 82
Bruce, James, 95, 99
Bryce, Capt. Robert, 11, 25, 26, 60
Buchan, Capt. Alexander, 89, 90, 93-95,
    98-100, 107, 109-111

Cameron, Capt. John, 78, 84, 86, 90, 93,
    100, 112, 120
Cavanagh, Capt. J., 105
Clark, Capt., 20
Clarkson & Co., 124, 125, 127
Clutha Shipping Co., 2, 5-7, 12
Connell & Co., C., 23
Connon, Capt., 20
Corsar & Sons, D., 74, 79
Crawford, W. & J., 20
Cundiff, Carroll, 128, 130

Dagwell, Capt. E., 82, 87
de Cloux, Capt. Reuben, 133, 144
Desmond, Mr Shaw, 151
Devitt & Moore, 102
Dix, Capt., 21
Dixon, Capt., 69
Dobson, Capt., 22
Duncan, Capt., 34

Duncan & Co., George, 30
Dundee Shipbulders' Co., 23

Eckener, Capt. Hugo, 154
Erikson, Capt. Gustaf, 90, 124-126, 128,
    136, 137, 140, 141, 147, 152, 160,
    161, 173, 177, 187, 188, 189
Eriksson, Capt. Isidor, 127, 131
Eriksson, Capt, Karl J. 142
Erskine, Mr, 73

Fernie & Sons, W.H., 92
Forrester, Mr J., 17
Fredericksson, J., 152, 162
Fullerton, Capt., 30
Fullilove, Capt. George, 84, 120-123
Gomm, Capt., 17, 21
Goodwin, Norman, 70
Graf Zeppelin, German airship, 154
Granith, Capt. 168

Hägerstrand, Capt. Ivar, 139
Hamburg Amerika Line, 177
Hamilton & Co., William, 62, 74
Hardie, Mr James, 1, 4-8, 14, 17, 18, 23,
    137
Hardie & Co., J., 1, 4, 24, 26, 28, 36, 38,
    79, 104, 123, 125, 174, 185
Hardie, Mr Thomas, 1, 2, 6, 104
Harrold Bros., 8-10
Hay, Mr J., 20
Heggie, Mr Colin, 166
Henderson, D. & W., 5, 23
Howie, Capt., 18
Hunt, Mr Cyril, 149, 150
Irving, Mr William, 51

Jansen, Capt. E.H., 140, 149, 150
Jarvis, Capt. J.C., 23
Johnstone, Mr William, 51
Jones, Capt., 21, 60, 78

Kavanagh, Capt. J., 105

Keir, Mr John, 114
King & Co., J.J., 188

Lancaster Shipowners' Co., 17
Law & Co's Shire Line, Thomas, 70, 78
Learmont, Capt. James, 54
Leman, Capt., 185
Lindfors, Capt. Harald, 151, 152, 155,
 161, 162, 164
Lindholm, Capt. R., 147 158, 160
Lloyds of London, 53, 117
Lowe, Capt. Charles, 50, 51, 55, 56, 58,
 64, 69
Lowe, Mrs Eleanor (wife of Charles) 52
Lubbock, Basil, 16
Luckner, Count von, 97
Lyne, Mr Harvey, 188

McCleve, Capt., 16
McCoy, Mr, 27, 28
McDonald, Capt., 11
McDonald, Mr, 114
McMillan, Capt., 60, 74-79, 101
McNeil, Capt., 24, 36
McRae, Duncan, 51, 84, 91, 107, 119
McRae, Mr Ian, 176, 179
Malcolm, Capt., 21
Mason, Capt., 17, 36
Masterton, Mr., 106
Ministry of Food, 187
Ministry of Transport, 188
Montgomery, Capt. Robert, 80, 81, 86,
 88, 123
Montgomery, Mrs (wife of Robert), 84,
 87
Morn, Capt. Uno, 185
Mylne, Mr A., 32

Napier, Mr James, 4
Neilson, Mr Hugh, 4
Nicol & Co., A., 52
Norddeutscher Lloyd, 125
Nourse & Co., James, 68

Öjst, Capt. Werner, 164

Peebles, Capt., 13

Petrie, Capt. A.J., 8, 10, 13
Petrov, Ivan, 65
Port Germein School, 170
Potter, W.H., 92
Price, W.R., 20
Pyne, Capt., 101, 120

Rasmussen, Mr Raoul, 152
Reid, Capt. David, 91
Reynolds, Capt., 17
Rile, James, 53, 56
Robertson, Capt., 12
Robson, Capt., 4, 8, 11, 14, 16, 35
Rogerson, Ralph, 89, 106, 109
Rose & Sons, George, 32
Rose & Co., 79
Russell, Mr Archibald, 1, 2, 4, 6, 29
Russell family, 170
Russell Ltd., Archibald, 104
Russell, Mrs Jackson, 1

Sage, Capt., 8, 11
Salmond, Thomas, 72
Scotts' Shipbuilding Co., 1, 23, 29
Sharp, Capt. William, 87
Shute, T.A., 79
Sjögren, Capt. Karl Gerhard, 144, 151
Sjögren, Capt. Mikael, 166-169, 172,
 177, 180, 181
Smith & Sons, George, 2
Söderlund, Capt., 183
Sommarlund, Capt. Paul, 152, 181-183,
 188
Souml, Victor, 93, 95
Steven, Capt., 16, 17, 33, 34, 60, 67, 68
Stewart & Co., J., 100
Stewart, W., 99
Swan, Hunter & Wigham Richardon Ltd.,
 187
Swinton, Capt., 69, 70, 73, 90

Thomas & Co., R., 87
Thomson, J. & J., of Glasgow, 11
Thomson, Capt., 86
Thompson, Mr, 76
Tilbrook, Mr Ron, 176, 177, 179, 180
True, Capt., 10

Tutton, Mr M., 20

Underhill, Harold, 189
United Towing Co., 182

Wakeham, Capt. W., 105
Walker, Capt., 17
Wallace, George, 4
Watson, Francis, 4
Watson, Capt. David, 30

Watson, Capt., 120
Williams, Capt. David, 187
Williams, Capt., 12, 60
Williamson, Capt., 18, 19
Wingate, Birrell & Co., 4
Windram & Co., G., 82
Woodget, Capt., 7
Wyness, Capt., 17

Young, Mr Richard, 182

Index of Ships

Aberlemno, 19
Abraham Rydberg, 165
Admiral Karpfanger, 177
Albuera, 16, 17, 21, 36
Alert, 165
Almora, 74, 80
Archibald Russell, 1, 23-25, 32, 33, 37,
    38, 40, 43, 47, 49-52, 54-58, 60, 61,
    62, 64, 65, 68, 69, 70, 72-79, 82, 84,
    92, 94, 95, 97-102, 105, 107, 109-
    114, 117, 118, 120, 122-125, 127,
    128, 130, 131, 133, 134, 136, 137,
    139, 140, 143, 144, 146, 147, 151,
    152, 154, 155, 157, 161-163, 165,
    166, 168, 169, 171, 172, 174-177,
    180-183, 185-188
Arcona, 77
Arctic Stream, 69
Arranmore, 81
Asia, 3
Austrasia, 126
Avoka, 67, 68

Baltimore, 14
Banffshire, 70,
Belfast, 75, 146
Bellands, 187
Bellhouse, 166
Bengairn, 94
Brambletye, 19-21, 74
Brecknockshire, 97
Brenda, 54
Brilliant Star, 51
British Isles, 54
British Yeoman, 97
Buteshire, 70

C.B. Pederson, 161
Caldergrove, 74, 101
California, 144
Canterbury, 75
Cardonia, 94
Carmen, 152

Celtic Burn, 102
Charles Gounod, 97
Chiltonford, 74, 79-82
Chrysomene, 92
Cimba, 52
Clevedon, 90-92, 105, 112, 118, 120, 123
Colonial Empire, 30
Corinthic, 60
Corunna, 16, 23, 35, 36
City of London, 3
City of Dublin, 3
City of Calcutta, 3
City of Oxford, 3
City of Manchester, 3
County of Caithness, 89
Crown of India, 89
Cutty Sark, 15, 16, 25, 99, 122, 123
Cressida, 2
Dallam Tower, 7, 17-19, 160
Dee, 98
Dolbadarn Castle, 102
Dorothy H. Sterling, 147
Dumfriesshire, 70, 90
Dunkerque, 54
Die Reine, 64

Elfrieda, 90
Elginshire, 79
Englishman, 182
Eudora, 8, 80

Fairport, 74, 80
Falkirk, 100
Fasholt, 148
Ferreira, 99
F. McCauly, 130
Forthbank, 52
Francesco C., 77

Galgate, 88, 94
Garthpool, 146
Glenalvon, 8
Globe, 70

Goodrich, 102
Grace Harwar, 125

Helgoland, 68
Herzogin Cecilie, 125, 133, 144, 146,
    152, 165, 180
Herzogin Sophie Charlotte, 69
Hinemoa 75
Hougomont, 23-25, 29, 50, 51, 55, 56, 58,
    74, 75, 85, 91, 102, 104, 105, 112,
    113, 119, 120, 123, 125, 128, 140,
    148-151, 157-160, 165, 168, 180
Inch Colm, 5
Inch Keith, 5, 7, 13, 16
Inch Kenneth, 5
Inch Marnock, 4, 5, 7-11
Inch Moan, 5, 13
Inch Murren, 5, 7, 10
Invercoe, 87
Inveresk, 89
Invergarry, 88, 100
Invermay, 60
Inverlyon, 94

John Hardie, 62, 64, 74, 91
Juteopolis, 79, 80

Kildalton, 74, 82, 87, 90
Kilmallie, 79, 100
Killoran, 74, 78, 82, 85, 91, 100, 101,
    105, 112-114, 117, 120, 122, 123,
    125, 140, 148, 157, 174, 175, 182
Kilmeny, 74, 78, 91, 105, 112-114, 118,
    120-124
Kirkcudbrightshire, 100
Kron Prinz Wilhelm, 87

La Plata, 53
Lapland, 88
L'Avenir, 126, 168, 174, 176, 177
Lawhill, 23, 125
Lime Branch, 77
Loch Broom, 78
Loch Lomond, 52
Loch Torridon, 8, 52

Manga Reva, 28

Marlborough Hill, 122
Maori, 70
Mary Ada Short, 87
Mataura, 13
Medway, 79, 102, 187
Melbourne, 162
Merchant, 77
Mersey, 76, 187
Monarch, 124
Monkbarns, 74, 79, 80, 82, 88
Monte Bianco, 133
Morayshire, 70
Moshulu, 10
Mount Stewart, 79, 100
Möwe, 97
Mozart, 146, 166
Musselcrag, 74, 80
Myr Shell, 32

Nivelle, 16, 23-25, 55, 60, 62

Oceana, 61
Olivebank, 125, 164, 183
Orthes, 5, 7, 8, 11-13
Ortina Shell, 102
Osborne, 56
Owenee, 102

Padua, 166
Pamir, 126, 151, 162
Pangani, 77
Parma, 152
Passat, 126
Pegasus, 74, 79
Penang, 125, 146, 165
Perce, 97
Pinmore, 84, 97
Pommern, 125, 162, 174
Ponape, 126, 168, 175
Potosi, 54
President de Leeuw, 114
Prinz Eitel Fredrich, 87
Priwall, 166
Pyrenees, 23, 25-28

Queen Margaret, 25
Queen Elizabeth, 60

Ravenhill, 94
Riverford, 100
Romanov, 52

St. Clemens, 65
Salamanca, 2, 5, 7, 8, 10-12
Saragossa, 16, 23, 25, 29, 33, 34, 42
Seeadler, 97
Sunlight, 90
Sydenham, 11

T.A. Jolliffe, 85
Talavera, 2, 6-8, 10, 11, 14-16, 24
Thistlebank, 84
Thornliebank, 52
Thyboron, 172
Torridon, 52
Trevean, 100

Upomendi, 111

Vanquisher, 118
Viking, 97, 126
Vimeira, 16, 23, 33, 60, 65, 67, 68, 78,
79, 85, 88, 91, 100, 102, 106, 112,
113, 120, 123

Walton Hill, 117
Wanderer, 92
White Rose, 123
Willerby, 87
William Mitchell, 110, 116
Winterhude, 125, 174, 182
Wolf, 98
Wray Castle, 87, 100

Yatala, 10
Yallaroi, 52

Index of Cargoes

ballast, 25, 33, 58, 74, 106, 113, 114, 118,
128, 133, 137, 144, 146, 152, 155,
157
barley, 27, 50, 73, 81, 88
building rubble, 114
case-oil, 25, 26, 64
cement, 35
coal, 7, 19, 24, 25, 34, 50, 54, 55, 56, 64,
70, 73, 80, 82, 85, 99, 104, 105, 113,
114, 118, 142, 185
coke, 54
copper, 81
general, 33, 51, 95, 101, 122
grain, 7, 58, 73, 78, 104, 112-114, 118,
137, 148
guano, 50, 54, 127, 128, 185
jarra, 98
logwood, 105

lumber, 34
maize, 185
nitrate, 7, 54, 72, 77, 80, 86, 109, 110,
113
Oregon logs, 91
palm-oil, 90
patent fuel, 148
pig-iron, 81
railway sleepers, 98
saltpetre, 82
sandballast, 150
sugar, 50, 91, 185
sulphur, 120
timber, 74, 78, 81, 90, 1122, 113, 122,
137, 142
wheat, 50, 64, 77, 143 151, 157, 164,
174, 181, 182
wool, 52, 122